Around the World in your
Slow Cooker

Global-Inspired, Family-Friendly Recipes

VICTORIA SHEARER

FOX CHAPEL
PUBLISHING

Recipe Conversions

Use the following conversion chart for liquids and larger dry ingredient measurements. Since the masses of some dry ingredients (pastes, ground herbs, etc.) will be different depending on how they are manufactured, we have not included mass (grams) conversions for dry ingredients used in sizes smaller than 1 tablespoon. You should research the correct conversion for the exact ingredient you are using.

⅛ teaspoon = 0.6 mL	½ cup = 120 mL
¼ teaspoon = 1.2 mL	¾ cup = 175 mL
½ teaspoon = 2.5 mL	1 cup = 240 mL
1 teaspoon = 5 mL	1 fluid ounce = 30 mL
½ tablespoon = 7.5 mL	1 ounce = 28 grams
1 tablespoon = 15 mL	1 fluid pound = 500 mL
⅛ cup = 30 mL	1 pound = 453 grams
¼ cup = 60 mL	

© 2024 by Victoria Shearer and Fox Chapel Publishing Company, Inc.

Around the World in Your Slow Cooker is an original work, first published in 2024 by Fox Chapel Publishing Company, Inc. All rights reserved. No part of this publication may be reproduced, stored in a retrieval system or transmitted, in any form or by any means, electronic, mechanical, photocopying, recording or otherwise, without the prior written permission of the copyright holders.

ISBN 978-1-4971-0471-6 (paperback)
ISBN 978-1-4971-0472-3 (hardcover)

Library of Congress Control Number: 2024935763

To learn more about the other great books from Fox Chapel Publishing, or to find a retailer near you, call toll-free 800-457-9112, send mail to 903 Square Street, Mount Joy, PA 17552, or visit us at *www. FoxChapelPublishing.com.*

We are always looking for talented authors. To submit an idea, please send a brief inquiry to acquisitions@foxchapelpublishing.com.

Printed in China
First printing

INTRODUCTION

Who doesn't crave a tasty restaurant quality meal that practically cooks itself? As a former travel writer, I've had the opportunity to visit myriad countries throughout the world and experience the unique flavor combinations brought forth in the cuisines of a wide variety of cultures. In developing this book, I set out to revisit global slow-cooked culinary classics and convert them for use in the modern-day slow cooker, which has enjoyed a renaissance in the twenty-first century. Today's home cooks have never been busier, their lives filled with careers, families, friends, and hobbies. But that doesn't mean they don't long for the flavors experienced on their last vacation in Europe or that they aren't curious about undiscovered culinary treats from foreign lands they've only read about. Whether you are an armchair traveler or a seasoned globe-trotter, pairing your adventurous palate with a slow cooker and this book will take your whole family on a flavor-packed journey.

Since the discovery of fire, humans have been slow cooking. A time-honored technique, this moist heat cooking—cooking in a constantly moving environment of liquid or steam—is now known as braising (from the French word *braise*, meaning ember). A good braise relies on the combination of dry and wet heat: dry—a good browning sear first put on the meat in a frying pan; and wet—long, slow cooking at a low temperature in a small amount of liquid. From the South African *potjiekos*, the Persian *khoresh*, the Moroccan tagine, and the Indian curry to the first American hearth-cooked stew, braised food has been a culinary staple the world over for centuries.

The Rival Company's 1970 release of the Crock Pot® slow cooker revolutionized this slow cooking process. Today, all slow cookers, no matter the brand, are based on the same simple design. Low-wattage heating coils are sandwiched between inner and outer metal walls, wrapping around the sides and bottom of the slow cooker. A stoneware, metal, or clay insert, which holds the food, fits inside the slow cooker cavity. The coils heat up, the space between the inner and outer walls heats up, and the indirect heat is transferred to the insert, which cooks the ingredients slowly and steadily. These devices make traditional braising techniques accessible in every kitchen.

So get ready, get your passport, and go around the world in your slow cooker: to the Middle East for Lebanese Orange-Apricot Chicken (page 99); South

Tagine cookware slowly cooks a meal over wood charcoal. You can achieve similar textures and flavors in your slow cooker.

Africa for Cape Malay Lamb Curry (page 75); or India for Rogan Josh (page 50); or perhaps to France for Beef Bourguignon (page 44); Asia for Chinese Red Cooked Beef (page 53); or Great Britain for Currant-Glazed Corned Beef (page 72). Then head back to North America for some Autumn Harvest Pork Roast (page 117), Chuckwagon Cowboy Chili (page 14), or a sweet Strawberry-Blueberry Crumble (page 166).

Bon Appétit! Buon appetito! Guten Appetit! ¡Buen provecho! Enjoy your meal!

72

168

CONTENTS

Today's slow cookers come in a wide variety of sizes and styles.

SLOW COOKER SAVVY

I used four different models of slow cookers in developing and testing the recipes in this book:

- 6-quart (5.7L) programmable cooker with a temperature probe and spoon lid
- 5½-quart (5.2L) cooker with a stove-top searing insert
- a slow cooker with 2-quart (1.9L) and 4-quart (3.8L) interchangeable inserts
- 1½-quart (1.4L) cooker with a lid latch

The two larger slow cookers were great when cooking for six or more or when cooking a roast, ribs, or whole chicken or making soup. The small slow cooker worked wonderfully well for small amounts and sauces. The most versatile, however, and my personal favorite, was the slow cooker with the interchangeable inserts. The 4-quart (3.8L) insert was perfect for many recipes serving four to six; the 2-quart (1.9L) insert worked well for servings for two people, and also for vegetarian dishes. (Both of the smaller slow cookers also are great for dips or desserts to accompany your entrées.)

In my extensive testing, I found that the slow cookers all cooked much faster than the manufacturer's stated times for recipe conversions. I found that in most cases, one hour of conventional cooking equaled about four to five hours in the slow cooker on the "low" setting. If meat or poultry cooked for more than six hours, it was likely "falling off the bone" or shredding, both of which are fine for many recipes, like Pulled Pork Tenderloin (page 126) or Russian Beef Stroganoff (page 60) but are undesirable for Greek Pork Chops (page 110) or Herbed Chicken Dijon (page 91).

When it comes to slow cookers, size matters. The cooking insert should be a minimum of one-half full and a maximum of three-quarters full to allow the ingredients to cook in the amount of time stated in a recipe. Filling a slow cooker less than this will cause the ingredients to cook much faster, so it is important that you choose the right size slow cooker when making a recipe. Small slow cookers are offered in 1½-quart, 2-quart, 2½-quart, and 3-quart (1.4L, 1.9L, 2.4L, and 2.8L) sizes. Medium cookers come in 3½-quart, 4-quart, and 4½-quart (3.3L, 3.8L, 4.3L) sizes. Large slow cookers have 5-quart, 5½-quart, 6-quart, 7-quart, 8-quart, and 10-quart (4.7L, 5.2L, 5.7L, 6.6L, 7.6L, and 9.5L) capacities. Most of the appliances are reasonably priced. If your budget allows and you have the storage

My interchangeable 4-quart/2-quart slow cooker is no longer manufactured, but newer models perform similar functions. For example, some 6-quart slow cookers accept two 2½-quart inserts to allow greater versatility.

space, invest in a couple sizes of slow cookers for maximum versatility.

Multicookers have also become very popular in recent years because they allow you to execute a number of different cooking methods, including slow cooking. They are often significantly more expensive, however.

Slow Cooking Tips

These slow cooking tips will help ensure culinary success every time.

- **When converting recipes for use in a slow cooker, use half the liquid called for in the original recipe.** Liquids do not evaporate in a slow cooker and the condensation under the lid adds ½ to 1 cup (120 to 240mL) of liquid during the cooking process.

- **If you double one of the recipes in this book, use twice as many dry ingredients but only 50 percent more liquid.** Make sure you use a slow cooker that is half to two-thirds full when all the ingredients are added. The cooking time will remain the same.

- **Use fresh vegetables unless the recipe advises otherwise, cut them into uniform pieces, and add them at the proper times.** Canned or frozen vegetables will overcook. Cutting your vegetables into uniform pieces will ensure that they cook consistently

Fresh vegetables hold up better in the slow cooker than canned or frozen.

Buy fresh herbs; rinse, dry, and snip them; then transfer them to labeled zipper bags to freeze them for up to a year.

and evenly. Put tender vegetables, like asparagus or snow peas, into the slow cooker during the final hour of cooking. Root vegetables cook more slowly than meat, so put them in the bottom of the slow cooker and around the sides of the meat so they are closer to the heating element in the walls of the slow cooker.

- **Brown ground beef in a skillet on the stove and drain it in a colander before placing it in the slow cooker.** This will eliminate excess grease.

- **It's best to use uncooked pasta in your slow cooker and add it at the right time.** Cooked pasta doesn't hold up well in the long slow cooking process. When making lasagna or macaroni and cheese, the uncooked pasta forms the backbone of the dish and should be placed in the slow cooker at the very start. (Make sure you have plenty of liquid.) For a soup, add the uncooked pasta during the final 30 to 45 minutes of the cooking process.

- **Use evaporated milk and processed cheese instead of milk or cream and regular cheese when converting recipes for a slow cooker.** Dairy products may break down in the slow cooker— prolonged cooking causes fresh dairy to separate and curdle. You can, however, add milk or cream to "finish" a recipe, adding it only in the final 15 minutes of cooking. Use processed cheese instead of regular cheese unless you plan to add the cheese in the final few minutes of cooking.

- **Add seafood within the final 30 minutes to 1 hour of cooking.** Seafood doesn't take long to cook.

- **Stews and casseroles can be held on warm for up to two hours.** Dishes with fragile ingredients, such as seafood, dairy products, or pasta, should not be held.

- **Two hours on the "low" heat setting equals one hour on the "high" setting.** This conversion is useful if you want to cook recipes faster.

- **A well-stocked spice stash is a must, especially when creating ethnic cuisine from around the world.** There are many online options for sourcing unusual spices, and many spice manufacturers have brick-and-mortar retail locations, as well.

- **Use fresh or frozen-fresh herbs where possible.** Fresh herbs are used extensively to flavor the unique cuisines around the world. I buy bundles of fresh herbs when they are inexpensive and plentiful in the summer season, then I rinse and dry them, snip them, and transfer them to labeled zipper bags for freezing.

Frozen herbs will keep in the freezer for a year, are easy to measure, and add a jolt of flavor freshness that dried herbs simply can't muster.

- **If you do use dried herbs, use one-third to one-half the amount of fresh herbs called for in the recipe.** Dried herbs lose their potency over time, so use more if your dried herbs are older.

- **Stir-in herb pastes are fantastic time-saving, flavor-boosting ingredients.** These finely ground pastes (I most often use Gourmet Garden brand) last for months in the refrigerator and eliminate prep time spent mincing, chopping, and snipping. I always keep garlic and gingerroot stir-in paste in my refrigerator, but there are other single-herb stir-in pastes available, as well as ethnic herb and spice blends like Italian and Thai.

- **Store nuts in the freezer to prevent them from becoming rancid.** While dried fruits can be kept almost indefinitely in the pantry, only a few roasted nuts should be stored this way. I keep bags of chopped walnuts, pecans, macadamia nuts, pistachios, pine nuts, and sliced almonds in my freezer. If you are using them in a recipe, you can use them frozen. If you want to add them to salads or use them as a garnish, dry-toast them in a skillet over low heat.

- **Freeze grated citrus peel and citrus juices from overripe fruits.** Fresh citrus juices and grated peel are essential elements in the cuisine of many of the countries surrounding the Mediterranean Sea, but they can be expensive to source elsewhere. Your grocery store may sell "overripe" oranges, limes, and lemons for a fraction of the price. If the peel is still unblemished, grate the citrus and then freeze it in a

Countries in the Middle East and the Mediterranean Rim use a lot of dried fruits and chopped nuts, such as apricots, dates, pistachios, and macadamia nuts, in their traditional dishes.

labeled zipper bag. You can also squeeze the fruit and freeze the juice in small plastic containers. Keep small bottles of lemon juice and lime juice in the refrigerator at all times. If a recipe calls for a tablespoon of fresh lemon juice, it will always be at your fingertips.

- **Freeze unused pastes, sauces, and broths.** Many recipes call for small amounts of tomato paste, tomato sauce, or even pesto, leaving a lot unused in the container. I wrap unused portions of tomato paste in cling wrap, form a cigar-shaped roll, and freeze it. When I need another tablespoon of paste, I simply unroll the cling wrap and cut off what I need with a sharp paring knife. I freeze extra tomato sauce and pesto in an ice cube tray and store the cubes in labeled zipper bags. I store unused chicken, beef, and vegetable broth in ½-cup (120mL) plastic containers in the freezer. They defrost in the microwave in seconds.

- **Use sweet onions, like Vidalia or Walla Walla, in your recipes.** These mild, sweet-tasting onions contain more sugar than the stronger-flavored Spanish yellow onions. Because of the higher sugar content, buy only the amount you'd use within two weeks and keep them refrigerated.

- **Store shallots in the refrigerator.** Shallots, a distant cousin of the onion, store well for months in the refrigerator. Very important in most cuisines of the world, shallots have a mild flavor with a hint of garlic. If a recipe calls for shallots and you don't have them, use an equal amount of chopped onion and add a finely minced clove of garlic.

Use ready-made pastes to save time without sacrificing flavor.

Dos and Don'ts

The following dos and don'ts include some food safety best practices and tips to ensure that your meals are properly cooked and flavorful.

✓ **DO** defrost foods before cooking so that they reach a safe temperature quickly.

✗ **DON'T** delay the start time or cook frozen items. Bacteria will form.

✓ **DO** switch the temperature to the warm setting when food is cooked to hold it for up to two hours.

✗ **DON'T** hold food on the off setting for more than one hour after cooking.

✓ **DO** tip the lid away from the food when removing it, so the condensation liquid under the lid doesn't go into the slow cooker.

✗ **DON'T** lift the lid during cooking time to see how things are progressing. Each time you do, it takes the slow cooker 20 to 30 minutes to get back up to temperature, thereby increasing the cooking time. (When a recipe in this book indicates lifting the lid, I've already planned for increased cooking time.)

DO layer the ingredients as directed in the recipe.

✓ **DO** layer ingredients as directed in the recipe.

✗ **DON'T** stir ingredients during cooking unless the recipe calls for it.

✓ **DO** load the slow cooker with ingredients before turning on the heat.

✗ **DON'T** preheat an empty slow cooker insert.

DO tip the lid away from the food when removing it.

Proper ingredient preparation will ensure that everything cooks evenly, including in multicookers like this one (which have become more popular in recent years).

✓ **DO** reheat already cooked food on the stove before transferring it to a slow cooker to keep hot on the low or warm setting.

✗ **DON'T** reheat cold cooked food in the slow cooker on any setting.

✓ **DO** use a hot pad when transferring the insert or lifting the lid. It will be hot.

✗ **DON'T** wash the slow cooker insert until it comes to room temperature.

✓ **DO** place the slow cooker on an uncluttered countertop.

✗ **DON'T** use an extension cord to plug in a slow cooker. The power cord is made intentionally short to minimize danger from tangling, tripping, or dumping over the hot contents.

✓ **DO** transfer cooked food to a covered container before refrigerating.

✗ **DON'T** refrigerate cooked food in the slow cooker—the insert may crack.

DO place the slow cooker on an uncluttered countertop.

HEARTY SOUPS AND STARTERS

These soups are hearty enough to be the main event.
The starters are a great pre-dinner snack.

 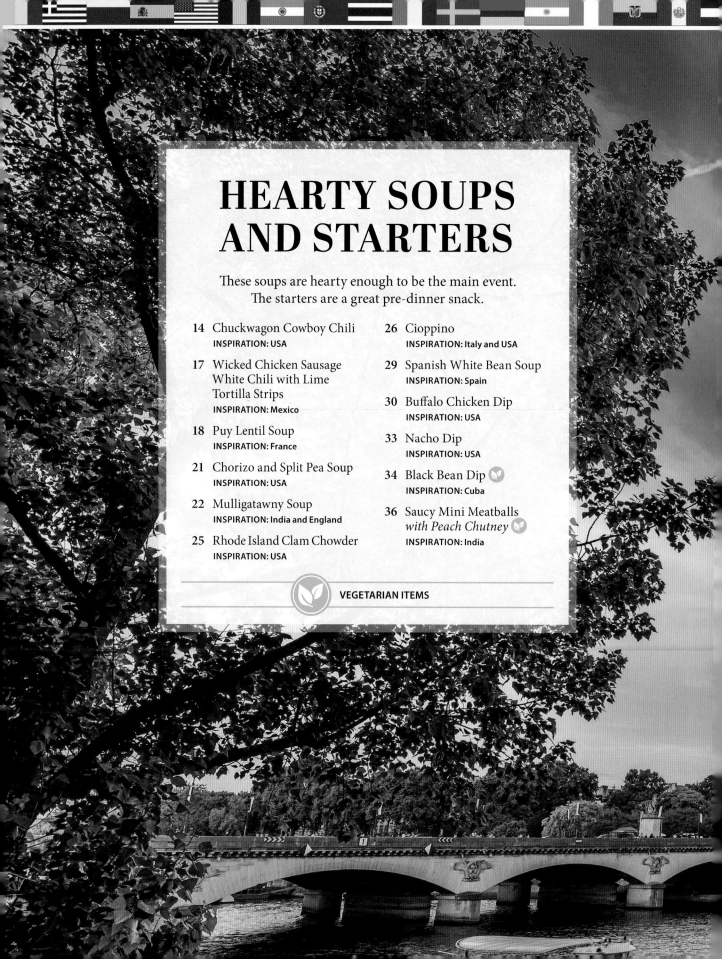
VEGETARIAN ITEMS

The Eiffel Tower reigns as the most iconic landmark in Paris, France.

Chuckwagon Cowboy Chili

Bison and grass-fed beef make this chili more like the thick and hearty type served on the chuckwagons out on the range in the Wild West. Today, most of the bison consumed in North America is farm-raised in Montana, Western Canada, Colorado, and the Dakotas.

Inspiration: USA | **Makes:** 14 cups (3.3L) | **Slow cooker time:** 6 to 7 hours

INGREDIENTS

- 2 tablespoons (30mL) olive oil, divided
- 2 cups (300g) chopped sweet onions, like Vidalia
- 1 red bell pepper, chopped
- 1 green bell pepper, chopped
- 4 teaspoons (18g) garlic paste or finely minced garlic
- 1 pound (454g) grass-fed ground chuck
- 1 pound (454g) ground bison

- 1½ pounds (567g) grass-fed chuck roast, excess fat removed and cut into ¾-inch (2cm) pieces
- One 14-ounce (397g) can petite-diced tomatoes
- 2 cups (480mL) beef broth
- One 11.5-ounce (326g) can vegetable juice (I used V8 Original)
- One 6-ounce (170g) can tomato paste with basil, garlic, and oregano
- One 4-ounce (113g) can mild green chilies

- 3 tablespoons (18g) chili powder
- 2 tablespoon (12g) ground cumin
- 1 tablespoon (6g) onion powder
- 2 tablespoons (30mL) Worcestershire sauce
- 3 tablespoons (45mL) soy sauce
- ¼ cup (60g) minced jalapeño peppers with seeds
- Shredded cheddar cheese
- Crispy tortilla strips

1. Place 1 tablespoon (15mL) of the olive oil in a large nonstick skillet over medium heat. Add the onions, bell peppers, and garlic and sauté them, stirring frequently, for 2 minutes, until the onions are sweated. Add the ground chuck and ground bison and sauté them until the meat has browned, about 5 minutes. Use a slotted spoon to transfer the meat and vegetables to a 5-quart (4.8L) slow cooker.

2. Discard the meat juices and wipe out the skillet with paper towels. Add the remaining 1 tablespoon (15mL) of oil to the skillet. Add the beef pieces and sauté them until browned, about 2 minutes. Use a slotted spoon to transfer them to the slow cooker.

3. Add the tomatoes, broth, vegetable juice, tomato paste, green chilies, chili powder, cumin, onion powder, Worcestershire sauce, soy sauce, and minced jalapeños to the slow cooker. Stir to mix the ingredients.

4. Cover the slow cooker and cook the chili on the low setting for 6 to 7 hours. Top each serving with shredded cheese and tortilla strips.

Try a variety of toppings for this hearty chili, such as shredded pepper jack cheese, minced onions, diced fresh tomatoes, or diced avocados.

Chicken sausage gives this chili a wickedly tasty kick.

Wicked Chicken Sausage White Chili with Lime Tortilla Strips

Wickedly spicy, wickedly tasty, this brothy chili is unlike its tomato-based cousins. The secret lies within the special chicken sausages.

Inspiration: Mexico | **Serves:** 8 | **Slow cooker time:** 4 hours

INGREDIENTS

- One ½-pound (227g) package spicy chicken sausage (see the tip box below).
- 1 teaspoon (5mL) olive oil
- 2 cups (300g) chopped sweet onions, like Vidalia
- 1¾ pounds (227g) boneless, skinless chicken breasts, cut into ½-inch (1.5cm) pieces
- One 15.8-ounce (448g) can great northern beans, rinsed and drained
- 1½ cups (83g) frozen gold and white corn
- 3 cups (720mL) chicken broth
- 1 teaspoon cumin
- 1 teaspoon dried oregano leaves
- ⅛ teaspoon cayenne pepper
- ¼ teaspoon salt
- 1 large burrito-size flour tortilla
- Olive oil spray
- Fresh lime juice
- Fresh cilantro, optional

1. Cut the casings off the sausages and chop them into ½-inch (1.5cm) pieces. Set them aside. Place the oil in a large nonstick skillet over medium heat. Add the onions and sauté them for 2 minutes, stirring frequently, until they're soft. Add the chicken and sauté the mixture for 2 minutes, stirring frequently, until the meat is browned. Add the sausage and sauté for 1 minute more, stirring constantly. Transfer the mixture to a 5-quart (4.8L) slow cooker.

2. Stir in the beans, corn, broth, cumin, oregano, cayenne, and salt. Cover the slow cooker and cook on the low setting for 4 hours.

3. While the chili is cooking, make the lime tortilla strips. Preheat the oven to 350°F (180°C). Coat the flour tortilla with olive oil spray and sprinkle it with fresh lime juice. Use a pizza cutter to cut the tortilla into thin strips. Place the strips on a nonstick baking sheet and bake for 5 minutes. Turn the strips with a firm spatula and bake them for 5 minutes more. Cool the strips and store them in a freezer-weight zipper bag at room temperature.

4. Serve the chili with lime tortilla strips and sprinkled with snips of cilantro.

The type of sausage used will influence your dish greatly. In this recipe, I used sausage made with smoked mozzarella cheese, roasted garlic, artichokes, and an array of spices. Mine came from a club store but you'll be able to find many similar varieties at your local butcher's shop or grocery store.

Puy Lentil Soup

Peppery French green lentils are the most delicate type of lentils. Originally grown in the Puy region of France, the lentils are actually small, dark, and speckled. They hold their shape well without becoming mushy but must cook longer than other types of lentils.

Inspiration: France | **Serves:** 8 | **Slow cooker time:** 9 hours

INGREDIENTS

- 1 pound (454g) French green lentils, rinsed and picked over
- 1 ham bone
- 1 cup (150g) chopped baby carrots
- 1 cup (150g) chopped sweet onions, like Vidalia
- 1 cup (225g) chopped celery

- 3 tablespoons (12g) minced curly parsley
- 1 teaspoon garlic paste or finely minced garlic
- 8 cups (2L) water, divided
- Two 14.5-ounce (411g) cans petite-cut diced tomatoes with garlic and olive oil, with juices

- 2 tablespoons (24g) sugar
- ½ teaspoon oregano leaves
- ½ teaspoon salt
- ¼ teaspoon black pepper
- 2 tablespoons (30mL) white wine vinegar
- 2 cups (60g) small croutons

1. Place the lentils, ham bone, carrots, onions, celery, and parsley in a 6-quart (5.7L) slow cooker. Whisk the garlic paste into 1 cup (240mL) of the water. Add the mixture to the slow cooker. Pour the remaining water into the slow cooker. Stir to mix the ingredients well. Cover the slow cooker and cook on the low setting for 4 hours.

2. Mix the tomatoes, sugar, oregano, salt, pepper, and vinegar together in a medium bowl. Add the mixture to the slow cooker and stir to combine. Cover the slow cooker and cook on the low setting for 5 hours more, until the lentils and vegetables are tender.

3. Remove the ham bone. Cut off any tender pieces of ham, then cut the meat into bite-size pieces and add it back into the soup. Sprinkle croutons atop each serving.

Green lentils are readily available at supermarkets and online. You can substitute regular lentils in this recipe if desired, but they will not hold their shape as well and may become mushy.

French green lentils are about a third of the size of regular lentils.

Chorizo sausage adds a spicy, smoky flavor to this split pea soup.

Chorizo and Split Pea Soup

Chorizo is fermented, cured pork sausage that originated in Spain and Portugal on the Iberian Peninsula. In the United States, you are more likely to find Mexican chorizo sausage, which is available uncooked or smoked. Whether you use Spanish, Portuguese, or Mexican chorizo, be sure it is the cured, smoked variety.

Inspiration: USA | **Serves:** 6 | **Slow cooker time:** 8 to 10 hours

INGREDIENTS

- 1 tablespoon (15mL) olive oil
- 8 ounces (227g) slim chorizo sticks, casings removed and thinly sliced
- 1 cup (150g) chopped sweet onions, like Vidalia
- ½ cup (53g) minced celery
- ½ cup (75g) minced carrots
- 1½ teaspoons garlic paste or minced garlic
- 8 to 10 ounces (227 to 284g) green split peas, rinsed and sorted
- One 32-ounce (1L) carton chicken broth
- 2 cups (500mL) water
- ½ teaspoon dried thyme
- Salt and pepper
- Croutons or oyster crackers

1. Place the olive oil in a large nonstick skillet over medium heat. Add the chorizo, onions, celery, carrots, garlic, and split peas. Sauté the mixture for 3 minutes, stirring frequently. Transfer the mixture to a 4-quart (3.8L) slow cooker. Add the chicken broth, water, and thyme and stir to mix well.

2. Cover the slow cooker and cook on the low setting for 8 to 10 hours, until the split peas are tender. Season the soup with salt and pepper to taste.

3. Puree the soup in batches in the blender. Return the pureed soup to the slow cooker and hold it on warm until you're ready to serve, up to 1 hour. Sprinkle each serving with croutons or oyster crackers.

If you want to use uncooked chorizo instead, remove the casings and cook the sausage in a nonstick skillet over medium heat, breaking it into small pieces. Drain the sausage on paper towels before adding it to the slow cooker.

Mulligatawny Soup

Originating in southern India, mulligatawny (or "pepper water") soup found its way to England and South Africa thanks to late-eighteenth century British military members and diplomats serving in the colonial services in the area once known as the Madras region. The most authentic way to serve this soup is with a side of plain or spiced rice.

Inspiration: India and England | **Serves:** 8 | **Slow cooker time:** 6 to 6½ hours

INGREDIENTS

- 4 pounds (2kg) cut-up chicken pieces, bone-in, skin removed
- Salt and black pepper
- 1 teaspoon curry powder
- ⅛ teaspoon ground cloves
- ⅛ teaspoon ground allspice
- ⅛ teaspoon cayenne pepper
- 1 teaspoon gingerroot paste or finely minced gingerroot
- 1 teaspoon garlic paste or finely minced garlic
- 2 tablespoons (28g) butter
- 2 cups (200g) sliced and quartered sweet onions, like Vidalia
- 2 tablespoons (16g) flour
- ⅓ cup (50g) golden raisins
- 1 apple, peeled, cored, and cut into ½-inch (1.5cm) pieces
- 1 green or red bell pepper, cut into ½-inch (1.5cm) pieces
- 1 cup (250g) peeled, chopped tomatoes
- 1 teaspoon (5mL) lemon juice
- Grated Parmesan cheese
- Snipped parsley

1. Place the chicken in a 4-quart (3.8L) slow cooker. Season it with 1½ teaspoons (9g) of the salt, curry powder, cloves, allspice, and cayenne pepper. Whisk the gingerroot and garlic pastes into 4 cups (1L) of water. Pour the mixture over the chicken. (If you are using minced gingerroot and garlic, sprinkle them over the chicken and then pour the water into the slow cooker.) Cover the slow cooker and cook on the low setting until the chicken is tender, 4 to 4½ hours.

2. Remove the chicken from the slow cooker and place it on a plate to cool. Pour the chicken broth through a fine-mesh strainer into a large bowl. Measure the broth, then add water until it measures 6 cups (1.5L) total. Pour the broth back into the slow cooker, then cover it and set the temperature to warm.

3. Melt the butter in a large nonstick skillet over medium heat. Add the onions and sauté them, stirring frequently, for 4 minutes or until they are soft. Stir the flour into the onions. Remove 1 cup (240mL) of warm broth from the slow cooker and gradually pour it into the skillet, stirring constantly. Transfer the onion mixture to the slow cooker and re-cover it.

4. With clean hands, remove the cooked chicken from the bones, discarding any remaining skin or grizzle. Chop the chicken into bite-size pieces. Add the chicken, raisins, apples, bell peppers, and tomatoes to the slow cooker. Cover the slow cooker and cook on the low setting for 2 to 2½ hours, until the flavors marry. Add the lemon juice and season the soup with salt and pepper to taste.

5. Serve in large shallow bowls, sprinkling the top with Parmesan cheese and parsley.

Mulligatawny soup originating in southern India contains lentils, but no meat. The English version evolved to include chicken or beef, but eliminated the lentils.

The rich, flavorful broth of Rhode Island's take on clam chowder elevates this soup to a class by itself.

Rhode Island Clam Chowder

Most folks have tasted creamy New England clam chowder and probably have at least heard of the tomato-red Manhattan version. But unless you have lived or vacationed in Rhode Island, chances are you have yet to discover the tasty clear-broth chowder so cherished in the tiny state. The essential ingredient for authentic Rhode Island chowder is quahogs, large hard-shelled clams with a distinctively briny taste. Quahogs are tough, so the clams must be chopped and cooked for a long period of time. Since fresh chopped quahogs are difficult to find if you're not on the Atlantic coast and preserved clams maintain their texture well in the slow cooker, I've substituted frozen or canned chopped clams and whole baby clams instead. (See the tip box below.)

Inspiration: USA | **Makes:** 10 cups (2.4L) | **Slow cooker time:** 6½ hours

INGREDIENTS

- 6 slices bacon, cut into ½-inch (1.5cm) pieces
- 1½ cups (225g) chopped sweet onions, like Vidalia
- 3 cups (975g) peeled, diced Yukon Gold potatoes
- Three 8-ounce (227g) bottles clam juice
- 3 cups (720mL) chicken broth
- 3 tablespoons (2g) snipped fresh dill
- 2 teaspoons black pepper
- 1 teaspoon salt
- 1 dash cayenne pepper
- 1 pound (454g) flash-frozen clam meat *or* three 6-ounce (179g) cans chopped clams plus one 10-ounce (284g) can whole baby clams, drained

1. Fry the bacon in a large nonstick skillet over medium heat until crispy. Remove it with a slotted spoon and drain it on paper towels. Discard all but 1 tablespoon (15mL) of the bacon grease. Add the onions and sauté them until browned, about 5 minutes. Transfer the onions and bacon to a 4-quart (3.8L) slow cooker. Add the potatoes, clam juice, broth, dill, pepper, salt, and cayenne pepper, then stir to combine.

2. Cover the slow cooker and cook on the low setting for 6 hours. Stir in the clams. Re-cover the slow cooker and cook on the low setting for 30 minutes more. Serve immediately or keep on the warm setting for up to 1 hour.

If you do have access to fresh quahogs, use 1 quart (900g) of chopped clams with the juices reserved (you can substitute the juices for some of the bottled clam juice). Add the chopped quahogs after 4 hours of cooking the broth and cook for 2½ hours more.

Cioppino

The word "cioppino" comes from the Ligurian language's "*ciuppin*," which is the name of a classic seafood soup from the Italian region of Liguria. Flavored with garlic, herbs, and a tomato-wine sauce, it was similar in flavor to today's American version of cioppino but with less tomato. Italian-Americans who fished off of Meiggs' Wharf in San Francisco in the late 1800s are credited with developing present-day cioppino. Legend has it that when a fisherman came back empty-handed, he walked around the wharf asking the other more fortunate fishermen to "chip in, chip in" and share some of their catch. Cioppino is a combination of fish, shrimp, and shellfish with fresh tomatoes in a wine sauce.

Inspiration: Italy and USA | **Serves:** 4 to 6 | **Slow cooker time:** 6½ to 8½ hours

INGREDIENTS

- 1 tablespoon (15mL) olive oil
- 1 cup (150g) chopped sweet onions, like Vidalia
- 2 tablespoons (8g) garlic paste or finely minced garlic
- Two 14.5-ounce (411g) cans diced tomatoes with basil, oregano, and garlic, plus juices
- Three 14.5-ounce (411g) cans chicken broth

- 1 dash hot sauce
- 1 cup (240mL) full-bodied red wine, like Shiraz or Zinfandel
- ¼ cup (5g) snipped fresh basil
- 3 bay leaves
- 1 pound (454g) large shrimp, peeled and deveined
- One 8-ounce (227g) can fresh lump crabmeat

- ½ to ¾ pound (227 to 340g) bay scallops
- ½ to 1 pound (227 to 454g) firm white fish, such as halibut, snapper, or grouper
- Salt and freshly ground black pepper
- Freshly grated Parmesan cheese
- ¼ cup (6.5g) snipped fresh parsley
- Crusty artisan bread

1. Place the oil in a large nonstick skillet over medium heat. Add the onions and sauté them until they're softened, stirring frequently, for about 2 minutes. Add the garlic and sauté the mixture, stirring constantly, for 1 minute.

2. Transfer the onion mixture to a 5-quart (4.8L) slow cooker. Add the tomatoes, broth, hot sauce, wine, basil, and bay leaves, then stir to combine. Cover the slow cooker and cook on the low setting for 6 to 8 hours, until the broth is rich and hot.

3. Add the shrimp, crabmeat, bay scallops, and fish. Cover the slow cooker and cook on the high setting for 20 minutes or until the shrimp turn pink and the fish and scallops turn opaque. (Do not overcook.) Remove the bay leaves and season the soup with salt and pepper to taste.

4. Serve the cioppino in large, shallow soup bowls. Sprinkle each serving with Parmesan cheese and parsley. Serve with artisan bread slices for dipping in the flavorful sauce.

Even a landlubber will love this exquisitely flavored Italian fish stew.

At the first sign of autumn, this hearty ham and navy bean soup begs to make its debut.

Spanish White Bean Soup

Many brands (most notably Goya and Badia) make a *sazón* (seasoning) blend of coriander, annatto, salt, garlic, dehydrated onion, paprika, and other Spanish spices. You can usually find these mixes in the Spanish section of your supermarket or at a Spanish grocery, but if you have trouble, they're available through online retailers, as well.

Inspiration: Spain | **Serves:** 8 to 10 | **Slow cooker time:** 6 to 8 hours

INGREDIENTS

- One 1-pound (454g) package dried navy beans
- 1 tablespoon (15mL) olive oil
- ½ pound (227g) ham, finely chopped
- ½ cup (75g) finely chopped sweet onions, like Vidalia
- ½ cup (25g) finely chopped peeled carrots
- ½ cup (113g) finely chopped celery
- 1 bunch fresh kale, washed, spun dry, and finely chopped
- 2 teaspoons garlic paste or finely minced garlic
- One 14.5-ounce (411g) can chicken broth
- ½ teaspoon crushed red pepper flakes
- 1 teaspoon (5mL) hot sauce
- 1 bay leaf
- ½ teaspoon white pepper
- 1 packet sazón (I use Goya or Badia)

1. Sort through the beans, discarding any broken ones. Place the beans in a large nonstick saucepan over medium-high heat. Add enough water to cover the beans by 2 inches (5cm). Bring to a boil, stir beans then turn off burner. Allow the beans to soften in the saucepan until most of the water has been absorbed, for about 1 hour. Drain the beans in a colander. Rinse the beans and then drain again. Transfer the beans to a 5- to 6-quart (4.8 to 5.7L) slow cooker.

2. Meanwhile, place the oil in a large nonstick skillet over medium heat. When the oil is hot, add the ham, onions, carrots, celery, kale, and garlic. Sauté the mixture, stirring frequently, until the vegetables are tender, about 4 minutes. Transfer the mixture to the slow cooker.

3. Add the chicken broth, red pepper flakes, hot sauce, bay leaf, white pepper, and sazón to the slow cooker. Stir to combine the ingredients, then add water until the slow cooker is three-quarters full.

4. Stir the ingredients, cover the slow cooker, and cook on the low setting for 6 to 8 hours. Remove the bay leaves before serving.

Navy beans are smaller and rounder than other white beans and maintain their shape during prolonged cooking better than other white beans.

Buffalo Chicken Dip

Legend has it that Buffalo chicken wings were first made as a late-night throw-together snack at the Anchor Bar in Buffalo, New York, by co-owner Teressa Bellissimo. This easy variation offers the same spicy kick as the original wings, but is bathed in creamy cheese dip.

Inspiration: USA | **Serves:** A crowd | **Slow cooker time:** 1 to 1½ hours

INGREDIENTS

- Two 8-ounce (227g) packages cream cheese
- 1 cup (240mL) spicy chicken wing sauce (I used Frank's RedHot Original Buffalo Wings Sauce)
- 3 cups (420g) finely diced rotisserie chicken
- 1½ cups (355mL) prepared ranch dressing
- 2 cups (450g) shredded sharp cheddar cheese
- 2 cups (450g) shredded mozzarella cheese

1. Place the cream cheese and buffalo sauce in a medium saucepan over medium heat. Cook the mixture, stirring constantly, until the cream cheese has melted. Transfer everything to a large bowl.

2. Stir in the chicken and ranch dressing, then transfer to a 1½- or 2-quart (1.4 or 1.9L) slow cooker. Cover the slow cooker and cook on the low setting for 1 to 1½ hours, until the dip has heated through. Stir in the cheeses. Reduce the heat setting to warm and serve the hot dip with your favorite dippers (I like Frito's Scoops and celery sticks).

Shredded cheese tends to curdle if cooked for long periods of time in a slow cooker. The cheese will melt quickly when stirred into the hot chicken mixture.

Since your guests will be serving themselves, make sure the dip is re-covered every time.

Use this recipe to top a pizza or pasta, put it in a wrap with crunchy lettuce, or use it to make quesadillas or nachos.

This nacho dip is a rich, hearty crowd-pleaser that packs a flavorful punch.

Nacho Dip

Tex-Mex at its best! Quick, easy, warm, and satisfying—you can also spread this dip over a bed of tortilla chips and pop it in the oven for a few minutes to make baked nachos.

Inspiration: USA | **Serves:** 12 to 16 | **Slow cooker time:** 2 hours

INGREDIENTS

- 1 cup (260g) leftover Chuckwagon Cowboy Chili (page 14) or Sloppy Joes (page 135), reheated
- One 8-ounce (227g) package cream cheese, softened
- 1 cup (200g) peeled, seeded, chopped tomato
- ¼ cup (60g) seeded, minced jalapeño peppers
- ½ cup (75g) minced red onions
- 1 cup (225g) shredded sharp cheddar cheese
- Tortilla chips

1. Place the chili or sloppy joes in a 1½-quart (1.4L) slow cooker. Spread the cream cheese on top, then add layers of tomatoes, jalapeños, onions, and cheese.

2. Cover the slow cooker and cook for 2 hours on the low setting.

3. Reduce the heat to the warm setting, stir to mix the dip ingredients, and serve from the slow cooker with the tortilla chips.

If you don't have any leftover chili or sloppy joes in your freezer, substitute 1 cup (260g) of refried beans.

Lightly salted tortilla chips, whether fried or baked, match perfectly with this flavorful dip.

Black Bean Dip

This dip is perfect on its own, but it also makes for a great addition to baked nachos. Place white tortilla chips on a large nonstick baking sheet in a single layer and spread the black bean dip over the top. Then add your choice of sliced olives, chopped onions, diced fresh tomatoes, or minced jalapeños. Sprinkle the whole thing with shredded cheese and bake for 5 minutes in a 400°F (200°C) oven.

Inspiration: Cuba | **Serves:** 6 to 8 | **Slow cooker time:** 2 to 3 hours

INGREDIENTS

- One 15-ounce (425g) can black beans, rinsed and drained
- 1 jalapeño pepper, finely chopped
- ¼ cup (40g) chopped sweet onion, like Vidalia
- ½ cup (120mL) thick and chunky medium spiced jarred salsa
- ¼ cup (60mL) sour cream
- 1¼ cups (140g) finely shredded Mexican cheese blend
- Tortilla chips

1. Place the beans, chopped jalapeño peppers, onions, and salsa in a 1½-quart (1.4L) slow cooker.

2. Cover the slow cooker and cook on the low setting for 2 to 3 hours.

3. Reduce the heat setting to warm and stir in the sour cream and shredded cheese. Serve immediately straight from the slow cooker or hold on the warm setting for 30 minutes. Make sure the cover is replaced between servings.

Cheese and sour cream tend to curdle if cooked in the slow cooker for a long time. Adding the ingredients at the end of the cooking cycle and reducing the heat to warm keeps the mixture creamy.

Try substituting 2 cups (360g) of the Cuban Black Beans (see the recipe on page 156) for the canned black beans.

Black beans are great sources of protein, fiber, B vitamins, and other healthy minerals.

This slightly spicy black bean concoction is great dipped right out of the slow cooker with your favorite dippers.

Saucy Mini Meatballs

These mini meatballs swim in a piquant Indian-inspired Peach Chutney sauce. For a main course, serve them, with the sauce, over Persian Rice (see the recipe on page 158).

Inspiration: India | **Serves:** 4 | **Slow cooker time:** 4 to 4½ hours

INGREDIENTS

- 1 cup (240mL) Peach Chutney (recipe on page 37)
- 1 cup (240mL) ketchup
- One 8-ounce (227g) can tomato sauce
- 2 teaspoons gingerroot paste or finely minced gingerroot
- ½ cup (104g) dark brown sugar
- 1¼ pounds (567g) lean ground beef
- ½ cup (30g) Panko breadcrumbs
- 1 tablespoon (2g) dried minced onions
- ½ teaspoon salt
- ⅛ teaspoon pepper
- ¼ cup (60mL) evaporated milk
- 1 egg, beaten

1. Mix together the chutney, ketchup, tomato sauce, gingerroot, and brown sugar in a medium bowl. Transfer the mixture to a 2-quart (1.9L) slow cooker.

2. Place the ground beef, breadcrumbs, onions, salt, pepper, evaporated milk, and egg in a large bowl. Use clean hands to mix the ingredients together well. Roll the beef mixture into 1-inch (2.5cm) balls.

3. Place the meatballs in the slow cooker, poking them into the sauce so that they are not overlapping each other but are entirely covered.

4. Cover the slow cooker and cook on the low setting for 4 to 4½ hours, until the meatballs are cooked through, and the sauce is rich and creamy.

Meatballs should be served hot in the sauce. Place fondue forks or toothpicks next to the slow cooker so that guests can spear their own.

Peach Chutney

A staple in Indian cuisine, this fruity, sweet-and-sour chutney should be made at the height of fresh peach season, then frozen in one-cup (240mL) canning jars for use throughout the year. It's perfect for making the Saucy Mini Meatballs on page 36. You can use two 1-pound (454g) bags of frozen peach slices, thawed, if you'd like to make the chutney out of season.

Inspiration: India | **Makes:** 8 cups (1.9L) | **Slow cooker time:** 3 to 4 hours

INGREDIENTS

- 1 tablespoon (14g) butter
- ½ cup (75g) chopped sweet onions, like Vidalia
- 1 tablespoon (14g) garlic paste or finely minced garlic
- 1 tablespoon (14g) gingerroot paste or finely minced gingerroot
- 1 tablespoon (15g) minced jalapeño peppers
- 1½ teaspoons mustard seed
- ¼ teaspoon curry powder
- 2 cups (416g) brown sugar
- 2 cups (480mL) cider vinegar
- 2 pounds (907g) fresh freestone peaches
- ½ cup (75g) golden raisins
- ¼ cup (40g) dried currants
- ½ cup (120mL) peach schnapps or peach nectar

This tangy chutney also makes a good condiment for grilled chicken, beef, or pork.

1. Melt the butter in a large nonstick saucepan over medium heat. Add the onions, garlic, gingerroot, and jalapeños and sauté for 3 minutes, stirring frequently. Add the mustard seed, curry powder, brown sugar, and vinegar, then stir to combine everything. Cook for 5 minutes, stirring occasionally.

2. Meanwhile, bring a medium saucepan of water to boil over high heat. Remove the pan from the heat and place it on a hot pad. Place each peach in the hot water for about 30 seconds. Remove the peaches from the water and peel each one. Cut the peaches away from the pit, then into ¾-inch (2cm) slices.

3. Add the peaches, raisins, currants, and schnapps or nectar to the vinegar mixture. Place the sauce in a 4-quart (3.8L) slow cooker.

4. Cover the slow cooker and cook on the low setting for 3 to 4 hours, stirring halfway through the cooking time, until the sauce is rich and thick. Use immediately to make the Sauced Mini Meatballs on page 36 or transfer the sauce to canning jars and refrigerate for up to 2 weeks or freeze until needed.

The remains of Bam Castle in Kerman, Iran.

BEEF, LAMB, AND VEAL

Slow cooking beef, lamb, and veal leads to the tender meat and savory, rich flavors celebrated in culinary traditions around the globe.

 VEGETARIAN ITEMS

This boldly spiced stew is one of the national dishes of Hungary.

Hungarian Goulash

It is said that "what pizza is to Italy and a burger is to America, the goulash is to Hungary." Hungarian goulash or *bográcsgulyás* means "herdsman's meat." Originally cooked in an iron kettle over an open fire, the dish could contain beef, pork, or lamb, as farmers and shepherds contributed what they could. Invading Turks introduced paprika to Hungary in the sixteenth century. The spice is now considered an essential ingredient in goulash.

Inspiration: Hungary | **Serves:** 6 to 8 | **Slow cooker time:** 6 hours

INGREDIENTS

- 1 teaspoon (5mL) olive oil
- 3 pounds (1.5kg) boneless chuck roast, cut into 1½-inch (4cm) pieces
- ½ teaspoon coarse salt
- ½ teaspoon cracked pepper
- 5 cups (500g) sliced sweet onions, like Vidalia
- ¼ cup (50g) brown sugar
- ¼ cup (60mL) fresh lime juice

- ½ teaspoon garlic powder
- 1 teaspoon hot ground mustard powder
- 1 tablespoon (15mL) Worcestershire sauce
- ½ cup (120mL) ketchup
- 2 teaspoons Hungarian sweet paprika

- 3 large Yukon gold potatoes, peeled and cut into 1½-inch (4cm) chunks
- 2 tablespoons (20g) cornstarch
- Salt and freshly ground black pepper
- Sour cream

1. Place the olive oil in a large nonstick skillet over medium heat. Sprinkle the meat with salt and pepper. Place the meat in the skillet in batches and brown it on all sides, about 3 minutes. Transfer to a 5 to 6-quart (4.7 to 5.7L) slow cooker. Top the meat with the onions. Whisk the brown sugar, lime juice, garlic powder, mustard powder, Worcestershire sauce, ketchup, and paprika together in a medium bowl. Pour the mixture over the meat.

2. Cook the meat on the low setting for 5 hours. Add the potatoes and cook for 1 hour more, until the potatoes are cooked through and the meat is tender when tested with a knife, but not falling apart. *(Hold on the warm setting for up to 1½ hours, if necessary.)*

3. Transfer the meat, onions, and potatoes to a large bowl. Place all but ¼ cup (60mL) of the remaining liquid in a small saucepan over medium heat. Place cornstarch in a small bowl. Whisk the remaining cooking liquid into the cornstarch to form a smooth paste.

4. Return the meat, onions, and potatoes to the slow cooker. Cover and reduce the heat to the warm setting. Add the cornstarch mixture to the liquid in the saucepan and whisk until thickened, about 10 minutes. Season with salt and pepper to taste. Place the goulash in a large, shallow serving bowl. Pour the sauce over the goulash and serve with sour cream on the side.

Hungarian-Style Paprika

Hungarian paprika is a spice made from grinding dried *Capsicum annum* peppers, commonly known as Hungarian peppers. The slender red peppers are about 4 inches (10cm) long. Most commercial Hungarian paprika is produced in the southern part of Hungary, notably around Kalocsa and Szeged. It is sold in a variety of sweetness and heat levels. An everyday staple in the Hungarian kitchen, nearly every dish has paprika as an essential ingredient. A shaker of paprika sits next to salt and pepper on most Hungarian dining tables.

This light, refreshing Persian stew showcases fresh rhubarb.

Persian Beef and Rhubarb Khoresh

A *khoresh* is a delicate, refined Persian stew that may be a combination of meat, poultry, or fish; vegetables; fresh or dried fruits; beans; grains; and even nuts. Traditionally simmered for a long time atop the stove, a khoresh converts wonderfully to a slow cooker. A good Persian cook uses whatever fruits and vegetables are in season. This light and refreshing beef stew showcases fresh rhubarb. Khoresh is always served atop saffron steamed rice, which Iranians call *chelow* (see page 158).

Inspiration: Iran | **Serves:** 4 to 6 | **Slow cooker time:** 5¾ hours

INGREDIENTS

- 1 tablespoon (15mL) olive oil
- 1½ pounds (680g) chuck roast cut into 1½-inch (4cm) chunks
- 4 cups (400g) thinly sliced sweet onions, like Vidalia
- 1½ teaspoons salt

- ¼ teaspoon black pepper
- 2 cups (50g) snipped fresh parsley
- ½ cup (15g) snipped fresh mint
- ¼ teaspoon ground saffron dissolved in 1 tablespoon (15mL) water or ¼ teaspoon turmeric*

- 1 tablespoon (14g) tomato paste
- 1 tablespoon (15mL) fresh lime juice
- 2½ cups (305g) peeled, diced rhubarb
- 2 tablespoons (24g) sugar
- 1 tablespoon (10g) cornstarch

*You can substitute turmeric for the saffron in this recipe without sacrificing the unique flavors of the dish. Although turmeric—a member of the ginger family— does not taste like saffron, it is inexpensive, will add the same distinctive yellow coloring to the dish, and adds its own subtle flavor.

1. Place the oil in a large nonstick skillet over medium heat. When the oil is hot, add the beef and sauté it, stirring frequently, for 2½ minutes. Add the onions and sauté the mix, stirring frequently, until the meat has browned and the onions are soft, about 2 minutes more. Transfer the beef and onions to a 4-quart (3.8L) slow cooker.

2. Add the salt, pepper, parsley, mint, saffron or turmeric, tomato paste, lime juice, and 1½ cups (375mL) of hot water. Stir to combine. Cover the slow cooker and cook for 4 hours.

3. Toss the rhubarb and sugar in a medium bowl. Add the mix to the slow cooker and stir the ingredients. Cover and cook for 1½ hours, until the meat is tender, and the rhubarb is cooked through but still firm.

4. Place the cornstarch in a small bowl. Stir in ¼ cup (60mL) of the liquid from the slow cooker to form a smooth paste. Stir the cornstarch mixture into the sauce in the slow cooker. Cover and cook for 15 minutes more, until the sauce thickens slightly. Taste the sauce and add more sugar to taste if it is too sour.

5. Serve immediately over steamed rice or reduce the heat to warm and serve within the hour.

Saffron

Saffron is a common ingredient in the cuisine of the Middle East, where it is plentiful. It originated in the ancient civilizations of Asia Minor, where it was used as a dye, as a perfume, and for medicinal purposes. Arab traders brought the spice to the Mediterranean in the tenth century. Actually the dried stigmas of the saffron crocus flower, saffron is entirely harvested by hand. It takes about 80,000 crocus flowers to yield 1¼ pounds (500g) of saffron. No wonder saffron is the world's most expensive spice. Saffron imparts an aromatic flavor and a golden color to dishes. Iran produces about forty-five percent of the world's saffron, and it is a signature spice in Persian cuisine.

Beef Bourguignon

This classic French dish, originating in the Burgundy district of France, demands a slow simmer in a full-bodied red wine sauce. The manner in which the stew is prepared is more important than using Burgundy wine. Any good-to-better red drinking wine will work. Pearl onions, mushrooms, and lardons (fried bacon) are traditional garnishes to the beef.

Inspiration: France | **Serves:** 8 to 10 | **Slow cooker time:** 5 hours

INGREDIENTS

- 6 slices bacon, cut into thin strips
- 1 cup (125g) flour
- 2 teaspoons salt
- 1 teaspoon black pepper
- 4 pounds (2kg) sirloin tip roast, cut into ¾- to 1-inch (2 to 2.5cm) pieces, fat removed
- Olive oil
- 2 teaspoons garlic paste or finely minced garlic
- 2 tablespoons (28g) tomato paste
- One 10¾-ounce (305g) can Campbell's golden mushroom soup
- One 1-ounce (28g) envelope dry onion soup mix (I used Lipton)
- 1¼ cups (296mL) Burgundy or other full-bodied red drinking wine
- 3 tablespoons (43g) butter
- 8 ounces (227g) button mushrooms, wiped clean, stems removed, thinly sliced
- 8 ounces (227g) baby bella mushrooms, wiped clean, stems removed, thinly sliced
- One 1-pound (454g) bag frozen pearl onions, thawed and drained
- 3 tablespoons (45mL) red currant jelly
- Snipped fresh curly parsley

1. Place the bacon in a large nonstick skillet over medium heat. Fry the bacon until it's crispy. Remove it from the skillet with a slotted spoon. Drain on paper towels. Store in a small zipper bag in the refrigerator until needed. Reserve the bacon grease in the skillet.

2. Place the flour, salt, and pepper in a large freezer-weight zipper bag. Add the meat in batches. Close the bag and shake it until the meat is well coated with flour. Transfer the floured meat to a dinner plate. Repeat with the remaining pieces of meat.

3. Heat the bacon grease in the skillet over medium heat. Brown the meat in batches. Transfer the browned meat to a 5½-quart (5.2L) slow cooker. (If the bacon grease cooks away, add 1 to 2 tablespoons [15 to 30mL] of olive oil to the skillet.)

4. Place the garlic paste, tomato paste, golden mushroom soup, onion soup mix, and wine in a medium bowl. Whisk until the ingredients are well combined. Pour the wine mixture into the slow cooker. Stir until the meat is well coated. (The wine mixture should just barely cover the meat. Add more wine if necessary.) Cover the slow cooker and cook on the low setting for 4 hours.

5. Meanwhile, melt the butter in a large nonstick skillet over medium heat. Add the mushrooms and sauté them, stirring frequently for 4 minutes. Add the onions and sauté the mixture for 1 minute more. Transfer the mixture to a covered container and refrigerate it until needed.

6. When the meat has cooked for 4 hours, add the reserved mushrooms, onions, and bacon to the slow cooker. Add the red currant jelly. Stir to combine the ingredients. Re-cover the slow cooker and cook for 1 hour more.

7. Serve with wide noodles, boiled new potatoes, or garlic bread. Sprinkle each portion with parsley before serving.

Considered the mother of all stews, beef bourguignon showcases tender chunks of beef in a rich red wine sauce.

This savory sauce is an unexpected mix of refined flavors and hearty texture.

Neapolitan Genovese

Virtually unknown outside of the Italian province of Campania, Genovese sauce is thought to have originated in the sixteenth century. Composed of onions, diced carrots, celery, and parsley stewed with a cut of beef or veal, a properly prepared Genovese is reminiscent of a fine French onion soup, but with the thick consistency of a Bolognese sauce. It is always served atop a tubular pasta.

Inspiration: Italy | **Serves:** 6 | **Slow cooker time:** 6¾ hours

INGREDIENTS

- 2 tablespoons (30mL) olive oil
- 3 pounds (1.5kg) chuck roast
- 3 ounces (85g) prosciutto, finely diced
- 3 ounces (85g) pancetta, finely diced
- 2 pounds (907g) sweet onions, like Vidalia, halved and thinly sliced

- ⅓ cup (35g) minced celery
- ⅓ cup (50g) minced carrots
- ⅓ cup (10g) snipped fresh flat-leaf parsley
- ½ teaspoon dried marjoram
- 1 teaspoon salt

- 1 teaspoon garlic paste or finely minced garlic
- ½ cup (120mL) dry white wine*
- 1 tablespoon (10g) cornstarch
- 1 pound (454g) ziti or penne pasta
- Grated Parmesan cheese
- Freshly ground black pepper

*It may seem like a very small amount of liquid is called for in this recipe, but when the onions cook down, they release a lot of liquid.

1. Place the oil in a large nonstick saucepan over medium heat. When the oil is hot, add the chuck roast and brown it on all sides, about 3 minutes. Transfer the roast to a 4-quart (3.8L) slow cooker.

2. Add the prosciutto, pancetta, onions, celery, carrots, parsley, marjoram, salt, and garlic to the saucepan and cook the mixture, stirring frequently, until the onions have softened, about 8 to 10 minutes. Transfer the onion mixture and juices to the slow cooker.

3. Cook on the low setting for 6 hours, until the meat is fork-tender. Remove the meat from the slow cooker and shred it. Mix the wine and cornstarch together in a small bowl. Add the mixture to the slow cooker and stir it into the sauce. Replace the shredded meat into the slow cooker. Cook on the high setting for 45 minutes, until the sauce is thick and darkish in color, and the onions are creamy.

4. About 15 minutes before serving, bring a large pot of water to boil over high heat. Add the pasta, reduce the heat to medium, and cook the pasta until it's al dente, following the package directions. Drain the pasta in a colander, reserving some of the cooking water. (Stir a little cooking water into the sauce if it is too thick.)

5. Place the pasta in a large bowl. Toss the sauce with the pasta so that the pasta is well coated but not drowning in sauce. Sprinkle the pasta liberally with Parmesan cheese and freshly ground black pepper and serve immediately.

Prosciutto di Parma

Prosciutto crudo (usually referred to simply as prosciutto) is uncooked Italian ham that has been salted and air-dried. Several regions of Italy have their own versions of prosciutto crudo, but one of the most special and well-known is Prosciutto di Parma, from the area around Parma, Emilia-Romagna. This also is the area where Parmesan cheese is made and the pigs raised in this area are partially fed the whey byproduct from the cheese-making process. The Parmesan whey in their diet regimen makes their flesh very mild and sweet and adds a slightly nutty flavor to the prosciutto. The pigs are kept in sheds and never let outside, which results in them being rather fatty.

Prosciutto di Parma is made from the hindquarters of the pig. The uncooked ham is salted (salt is the only additive allowed) and hung at room temperature or in a climate-controlled environment for at least eighteen months and up to two years. The production of Prosciutto di Parma is restricted by law to the area between the Tara and Baganza rivers, where the air and humidity have been deemed to be ideal.

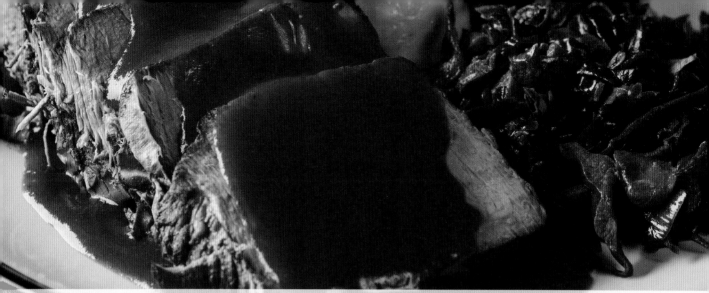

My version of German sauerbraten has more of a sweet kick.

Sweet and Sour Sliced Eye of Round

Eye of round roast is very lean, lacking the marbling of fat found in other cuts of beef. It needs to be braised while covered in liquid, which makes it the perfect cut to use in a slow cooker. Distinctive from German sauerbraten, or "sour roast," which is more sour than sweet, this eye of round is more sweet than sour. It is delicious served with dumplings or cabbage, but it makes a delicious pairing with Stovie Potatoes (see page 49).

Inspiration: Germany | **Serves:** 8 | **Slow cooker time:** 7¼ hours

INGREDIENTS

- 1 tablespoon (15mL) olive oil
- One 4¾- to 5-pound (2 to 2.5kg) eye of round roast
- 2 large sweet onions, like Vidalia, cut in half and thinly sliced
- 1 cup (240mL) ketchup
- One 12-ounce (340g) bottle chili sauce (I used Bennetts)

- ⅓ cup (80mL) red wine vinegar
- ¼ cup (52g) packed brown sugar
- 2 tablespoons (30mL) Worcestershire sauce
- 1 teaspoon dry mustard
- 1 teaspoon oregano leaves
- 1 teaspoon black pepper
- ½ teaspoon garlic powder

- ½ teaspoon chili powder
- ½ teaspoon ground cloves
- ¼ teaspoon ground nutmeg
- 1 teaspoon (5mL) hot sauce
- 2 cups (500mL) water
- 1 tablespoon (10g) cornstarch

1. Place the olive oil in a large nonstick saucepan over medium heat. Add the roast and sear it on all sides, about 2 minutes. Transfer the seared roast to a 5- to 6-quart (4.8 to 5.7L) slow cooker. Top the roast with the onions.

2. Whisk the ketchup, chili sauce, vinegar, brown sugar, Worcestershire sauce, dry mustard, oregano, pepper, garlic powder, chili powder, cloves, nutmeg, and hot sauce together in a large bowl. Stir in the water. Pour the mixture over the roast in the slow cooker. Cover and cook on low for 6 hours, until the roast has cooked through but is still firm.

3. Remove the roast from the slow cooker. Cover it with aluminum foil. Whisk the cornstarch with 2 tablespoons (30mL) of the cooking liquid. Add the cornstarch mixture to the slow cooker and whisk to combine. Re-cover the slow cooker, raise the heat to the high setting, and cook the sauce for 15 minutes.

4. Cut the roast into thin slices. Return the slices to the slow cooker, reduce the heat to the low setting, re-cover it, and cook for 1 hour more, until the beef is fork-tender.

5. Serve the beef slices topped with the onions and sauce.

Stovie Potatoes

Stovies are a traditional Scottish dish, slowly cooked in a covered cast-iron skillet. Good stovies must be cooked for several hours without them burning onto the bottom of the skillet. Tradition mandates that the lid must never be lifted during the cooking time. Perfectly suited for conversion to a slow cooker, these thinly sliced, seasoned potatoes cook for several hours while bathed in melted butter.

Inspiration: Scotland | **Serves:** 4 | **Slow cooker time:** 6 to 8 hours

These potatoes are creamy comfort food.

INGREDIENTS

- ½ cup (45g) grated Parmesan cheese
- ¼ cup (30g) flour
- ¼ teaspoon seasoning blend
- ¼ teaspoon black pepper
- 6 tablespoons (85g) plus 1 teaspoon (5g) butter, divided
- 3 large Yukon Gold potatoes
- Salt

1. Mix the cheese, flour, seasoning blend, and pepper together in a medium bowl. Grease the bottom and sides of a 2-quart (1.9L) slow cooker with 1 teaspoon (5g) of the butter.

2. Working with one potato at a time, peel the potato and cut it into ¼-inch (6mm) slices. Dredge the potato slices in the cheese-flour mixture, making sure both sides are well coated. Place the slices in an overlapping layer on the bottom of the slow cooker. Sprinkle the layer with salt to taste. Divide the butter into three equal parts. Cut one portion of butter into eighteen small pieces. Sprinkle the butter on top of the potatoes.

3. Repeat with two more layers of the coated potatoes, salt, and butter. Sprinkle any remaining cheese-flour mixture on top of the potatoes. Cover the slow cooker and cook on the low setting for 6 to 8 hours, until the potatoes are cooked through and bubbly, but not mushy.

> *Some authentic Stovie potatoes are layered with onions, as well. If you'd like to add onions, thinly slice a large sweet onion, such as a Vidalia. Sauté the onion slices in 1 tablespoon (14g) of butter in a large nonstick skillet for about 3 minutes, until the onions are soft. Divide the onions equally and place them on top of each potato layer.*
>
> *To serve 6 to 8, double the recipe, making six layers instead of three layers, and cook it in a 4-quart (3.8L) slow cooker.*

Rogan Josh

Originating in Kashmir, in northern India, rogan josh is a stew, usually made with lamb, which is indigenous to that country. Here in the United States, lamb is a bit pricey, so this version of the traditional highly spiced stew is made with beef. Every Indian family has its own recipe for rogan josh, usually handed down from mother to daughter over generations. The recipe gets its name from the rich, red color imparted by the copious amounts of ground hot red peppers. If you like your food really spicy, add more cayenne pepper. Serve with steamed white rice or Indian naan (flatbread).

Inspiration: India | **Serves:** 4 | **Slow cooker time:** 8 hours

INGREDIENTS

- 1½ teaspoons ground cardamom
- 2 bay leaves
- 6 whole cloves
- Salt and black pepper
- One 1-inch (2.5cm) stick cinnamon
- 1 teaspoon ground coriander
- 2 teaspoons ground cumin
- 4 teaspoons red paprika
- ½ teaspoon cayenne pepper
- 1 tablespoon (15mL) olive oil
- 1¾- to 2-pound (0.8 to 1kg) beef chuck, cut into 1-inch (2.5cm) cubes
- 2 cups (300g) chopped sweet onions, like Vidalia
- 1 tablespoon (14g) gingerroot paste or finely minced gingerroot
- 1 tablespoon (14g) garlic paste or finely minced garlic
- 1 cup (240mL) beef broth
- ¼ cup (18g) dried, sweetened coconut, divided
- ¼ cup (27g) slivered almonds, dry-toasted
- 1 cup (240mL) plain yogurt, divided

1. Place the cardamom, bay leaves, cloves, ¼ teaspoon of the black pepper, and the cinnamon stick in a small bowl. Set it aside. Place the coriander, cumin, 1¼ teaspoons of the salt, paprika, and cayenne pepper in another small bowl. Set it aside.

2. Place the olive oil in a large nonstick skillet over medium heat. Add the beef cubes and sauté them, stirring frequently for 2 minutes, until the meat is browned. Use a slotted spoon to transfer the beef to a 2-quart (1.9L) slow cooker.

3. Place the cardamom spice mixture in a skillet over medium heat and stir for 10 seconds. Add the onions and sauté them, stirring frequently for 2 minutes. Add the gingerroot and garlic pastes and sauté together for 30 seconds, stirring constantly. Add the coriander spice mixture and sauté together for 30 seconds more. Transfer the onion mixture to the slow cooker.

4. Add the broth, 2 tablespoons (9g) of the coconut, and the almonds to the slow cooker. Stir until all the ingredients are well mixed. Cover and cook on the low setting for 8 hours.

5. Reduce the heat to the warm setting. Stir in ½ cup (120mL) of the yogurt and serve within 15 minutes. Season with salt and pepper to taste. Sprinkle each portion with ½ tablespoon of the coconut and top with a dollop of yogurt.

Originating in Kashmir in India, the name "Rogan Josh" is believed to have come from the Hindu words for red or hot (*Rogan*) and for stew or braise (*Josh*).

The soy sauce in this recipe thickens and the sugar caramelizes, making the beef a deep mahogany color.

Chinese Red Cooked Beef

Red cooking, or *hong shao*, is a Chinese culinary technique that calls for meat to be quickly seared and then slowly simmered in a spicy broth. Supposedly, the "red" color comes from copious amounts of soy sauce in the broth. In this recipe, I've substituted ponzu sauce, a citrus-and-vinegar-flavored soy sauce, for a lighter, more flavorful broth.

Inspiration: China | **Serves:** 4 | **Slow cooker time:** 3 to 3½ hours

INGREDIENTS

- 1¾ pounds (794g) Angus skirt steak
- 1 tablespoon (15mL) olive oil
- One 1-inch (2.5cm) piece gingerroot, peeled and thinly sliced
- 3 scallions, halved lengthwise and cut into thirds
- ½ cup (120mL) ponzu sauce
- 1 teaspoon (4.5g) garlic paste or finely minced garlic
- 1 tablespoon (12g) sugar
- 1 cup (240mL) water

1. Cut steak the into pieces that will fit into a 1½-quart (1.4L) slow cooker. Place the olive oil in a large nonstick skillet over medium-high heat. When the oil is hot, add the steak, searing each side for only 15 seconds per side. Transfer the seared steak to the slow cooker.

2. Sprinkle the gingerroot slices and scallions over the beef. Whisk the ponzu sauce, garlic, and sugar together in a medium bowl. Whisk in the water and pour the mixture over the beef in the slow cooker.

3. Cover the slow cooker and cook on the low setting for 3 to 3½ hours, until the steak is medium-rare when tested with a sharp knife. Remove the steak from the slow cooker and cut it into ½-inch (1.5cm) slices. Serve immediately, drizzled with sauce if desired.

Gingerroot is actually the rhizome of a flowering plant, and it has a vibrant, aromatic flavor.

This brisket blends sweet and tart with savory.

Beef Brisket

As much as brisket is associated with the American South, it actually originated as a traditional kosher food in Jewish communities in Europe, where it was served on holidays like Hannukah, Shabbat, and Passover. (Brisket is found in the cow's front breast, making it kosher to consume.) When Jewish immigrants came to America, brisket came with them! Brisket is a tough, muscular meat that, when slowly cooked over a long period of time in this very simple sauce, transforms into an otherworldly taste sensation.

Inspiration: USA | **Serves:** 8 | **Slow cooker time:** 7 hours

INGREDIENTS

- 4 to 4½ pounds (1.8 to 2kg) beef brisket
- 1 tablespoon (15mL) olive oil
- One 14-ounce (397g) can cranberry sauce
- ½ cup (120mL) orange juice
- One 1-ounce (28g) envelope dry onion soup mix (I used Lipton)

1. Cut the brisket in half, crosswise, into two pieces. Place the oil in a large nonstick skillet over medium heat. When the oil is hot, sear both sides of each brisket piece, about 30 seconds per side. Transfer the brisket pieces to a dinner plate.

2. Mix the cranberry sauce, orange juice, and onion soup mix together in a medium bowl. Place one piece of brisket in a 5- to 5½-quart (4.7 to 5.2L) slow cooker. Spoon half the cranberry mixture over the brisket. Place the remaining piece of brisket on top of the other. Spoon the remaining cranberry mixture over the brisket.

3. Cover the slow cooker and cook on the low setting for 5 hours. Remove the meat to a cutting board. Slice the brisket against the grain into ¼-inch (6mm) slices. Return the brisket slices to the slow cooker, making sure they are covered with sauce. Re-cover the slow cooker and cook on the low setting for 2 hours more, until the meat is fork-tender but not shredding.

4. Serve with Sweet and Sour Baby Onions (see page 55).

Sweet and Sour Baby Onions

These small but flavorful onions are the perfect accompaniment for any slow cooker beef dishes, but they work especially well with brisket.

Inspiration: USA | **Serves:** 8 | **Slow cooker time:** 4 to 4½ hours

INGREDIENTS

- Two 1-pound (454g) bags frozen peeled white pearl onions
- One extra-large chicken bouillon cube
- 2 tablespoons (30mL) melted butter
- 2 tablespoons (30mL) white balsamic vinegar
- 1 tablespoon (12g) sugar
- Salt and freshly ground black pepper
- 1½ teaspoons cornstarch

1. Place the frozen onions in a 4-quart (3.8L) slow cooker. Crumble the bouillon cube into a small bowl. Whisk in the butter, vinegar, and sugar. Pour the mixture over the onions and stir to combine. Cover the slow cooker and cook on the low setting for 4 to 4½ hours. Add salt and pepper to taste, stir the onions, re-cover the slow cooker, and cook for 30 more minutes.

2. Strain the onions in a sieve placed over a small glass bowl. Place the onions in a serving bowl. Whisk the cornstarch into the onion liquid. Microwave the liquid until it thickens, about 1 to 2 minutes.

3. Pour the sauce over the onions and toss to combine. Serve with Beef Brisket (see page 54).

These onions have a solid but tender texture.

The warming spices used in this dish are classics when paired with beef and onion.

Beef and Onion Potjiekos

This not-quite-authentic interpretation of a South African *potjiekos* (see page 57) tastes even better when made a couple of days ahead of time and reheated.

Inspiration: South Africa | **Serves:** 3 to 4 | **Slow cooker time:** 5 to 5½ hours

INGREDIENTS

- 2 tablespoons (16g) flour
- ½ teaspoon paprika
- Salt and black pepper
- 1¾ pounds (794g) chuck roast, cut into 1½- to 2-inch (4 to 5cm) chunks
- 1 tablespoon (15mL) olive oil
- 1½ cups (225g) roughly chopped sweet onions, like Vidalia
- 3 tablespoons (45mL) red wine
- ¼ cup (60mL) beef broth
- 1½ tablespoons (21g) tomato paste
- 1 tablespoon (6g) grated orange peel
- 1 bay leaf
- ½ stick cinnamon
- 3 whole cloves
- One-half 1-pound (454g) package frozen white pearl onions, defrosted and drained

1. Mix the flour, paprika, ½ teaspoon of the salt, and ½ teaspoon of the pepper together in a small bowl. Place the beef chunks in a large bowl. Sprinkle with the flour mixture and toss until the beef is well coated.

2. Place the oil in a large nonstick skillet over medium heat. When the oil is hot, add the beef and chopped onions and sauté them until the beef has browned, about 3 minutes. Mix the wine, broth, and tomato paste together in a small bowl. Add the mixture to the skillet and stir it into the beef and onions, deglazing the pan of any burned bits of the flour mixture.

3. Transfer the beef mixture to a 2-quart (1.9L) slow cooker. Stir in the orange peel, bay leaf, cinnamon stick, and cloves. Cover and cook on the low setting for 4 hours. Add the pearl onions, stir them into the beef mixture, cover the slow cooker, and cook for 1 to 1½ hours more, until the beef is tender but not falling apart.

4. Remove the bay leaf and cinnamon stick. Add salt and pepper to taste before serving. Serve potjiekos with baked, boiled, or mashed potatoes, topping them with the flavorful gravy.

Potjiekos

Potjiekos (pronounced *poi-key-kos*) is a South African dish that is traditionally prepared outdoors in a potjie—a three-legged, cast-iron cauldron with a tight-fitting lid—over moderately hot coals on the ground. Similar to a stew, potjiekos—which literally means little pot (*potjie*) food (*kos*)—was brought to South Africa with early Dutch immigrants in the seventeenth century. (Holland ruled the Cape of Good Hope for 150 years.) Potjiekos differs from a stew in a few ways. Only a small amount of sauce liquid is added and the potjie is never stirred during the cooking process. The tight-lidded potjie creates a pressure-cooker effect, steaming the ingredients rather than boiling them. Since potjiekos is not stirred, the flavors of the individual ingredients remain distinct.

Authentic potjiekos is a strictly layered dish consisting of meat, vegetables, potatoes, and a seasoned sauce. Called "building the potjie," first the potjie, with some cooking oil, is placed over the coals. The meat is added and is seared and browned to lock in its juices. Next, the vegetables are added, layer by layer, with those requiring more cooking time on the bottom. Then, a sealing layer of sliced potatoes is placed on top of the vegetable layers. Finally, a small amount of highly seasoned sauce liquid (often beer or wine and Cape Malay spices) is poured into the cauldron around the edges of the potjiekos. The lid is tightly secured, and the ingredients slowly braise for several hours. The lid is never removed during cooking—to check on the progress, the cook would put an ear to the potjie, listening for slight bubbling sounds. This is called "listening to the potjie talk." Sounds of rapid boiling indicate that the coals are too hot.

A cast-iron pot over hot coals is the traditional tool used to make South African potjiekos.

This stew is the ultimate comfort food: it has savory flavors, tender meat, and creamy root vegetables.

Irish Stew

Irish stew evolved in the early nineteenth century during a period of extreme poverty. Even the poorest families managed to get the few ingredients it took to put together this hearty stew.

Inspiration: Ireland | **Serves:** 6 | **Slow cooker time:** 6 to 6½ hours

INGREDIENTS

- ⅓ cup (40g) flour
- 2½ pounds (1kg) sirloin tip roast or leg of lamb, cut into 1½-inch (4cm) pieces
- Salt and freshly ground black pepper
- 1½ pounds (680g) white new potatoes, cut in half
- 2 large leeks, white and light green parts only, cut in half lengthwise, washed, and cut crosswise into ¾-inch (2cm) pieces
- 1 large sweet onion, like Vidalia, cut in half and thinly sliced
- 1½ cups (360mL) beef broth
- 2 teaspoons garlic paste or finely minced garlic
- 1 teaspoon dried thyme
- 2 teaspoons (10mL) Worcestershire sauce
- Snipped fresh curly parsley

1. Place the flour in a large zipper bag. Working in batches of 5 to 6 pieces at a time, add the beef or lamb to the bag, close it, and shake it until the flour coats the meat evenly. Transfer the floured meat to a large plate. Season the meat with 1 teaspoon (6g) of the salt and ½ teaspoon (1g) of the pepper.

2. Place half the potatoes in the bottom of a 5- to 5½-quart (4.8 to 5.2mL) slow cooker. Top them with half the leeks and half the onions. Place the meat pieces on top of the vegetables. Layer the remaining leeks, onions, and potatoes on top of the meat.

3. Whisk the broth, garlic paste, thyme, and Worcestershire sauce together in a medium bowl. Pour the mixture over the ingredients in the slow cooker. Cover the slow cooker and cook on the low setting for 6 to 6½ hours, until the beef or lamb and potatoes are tender.

4. Place each serving in a large, shallow soup bowl. Season them with salt and pepper to taste. Top each with a sprinkling of fresh parsley.

Meals cooked in a cauldron over an open fire feature heavily in early Irish culinary tradition.

Irish Stew

Irish stew (*Stobhach Gaelach*) is a classic Irish peasant dish, originating in the eighteenth century during a period of famine and immense poverty. Rural Irish farmers raised sheep for wool and for milk, keeping them well into old age before committing them to the cooking pot. (Wool-bearing sheep and young lambs were far too valuable to sacrifice for dinner.) They also raised root vegetable crops. The primary component of early Irish stew, therefore, was mutton, usually on the bone from the neck or shank. The meat was very tough and strongly flavored and required long, slow cooking to make it edible. Only potatoes, onions, salt, and water were added to the mutton in the cauldron, where they simmered together for hours. Eventually other root vegetables, such as carrots, turnips, or parsnips, were added to the mix.

Irish immigrants to the United States found that sheep were not as plentiful as in Ireland, so beef became the preferred ingredient in their Irish stews. But the central elements of the dish remain unchanged today.

Russian Beef Stroganoff

The amazing commingling of horseradish and mustard is a Russian-inspired marriage made in heaven. The addition of sour cream just before serving mellows the tangy sauce and makes it creamy. Russians typically eat stroganoff with potato straws. Serve this dish with wide egg noodles.

Inspiration: Russia | **Serves:** 6 | **Slow cooker time:** 8 hours

INGREDIENTS

- 6 tablespoons (85g) butter, divided
- 3 pounds (1.5kg) beef stew meat, cut into 2-inch (5cm) chunks
- Salt and freshly ground black pepper
- 4 teaspoons garlic paste or finely minced garlic
- 4 cups (600g) chopped sweet onions, like Vidalia
- 1 cup (150g) finely chopped baby carrots
- 1 cup (237mL) beef broth
- 1 cup (237mL) white wine
- 2 bay leaves
- 3 tablespoons (23g) flour
- ½ cup (120mL) prepared horseradish
- 2 tablespoons (30mL) Dijon mustard
- ½ cup (120mL) sour cream
- Fresh snipped parsley

1. Melt 4 tablespoons (57g) of the butter in a large nonstick skillet over medium heat. Brown half the meat, about 30 seconds per side. Use a slotted spoon to remove the meat to a large plate. Repeat this process with the remaining meat. Season the meat with salt and pepper to taste.

2. Add the garlic, onions, and carrots to the skillet and sauté them, stirring occasionally, for 5 minutes. Season the mixture with salt and pepper to taste. Transfer the vegetables to a 4-quart (3.8L) slow cooker. Place the browned meat on top of the vegetables.

3. Mix the broth and wine together in a 2-cup (474mL) measuring cup. Pour the mixture over the beef and vegetables in the slow cooker. Tuck the bay leaves into the meat mixture. Cover the slow cooker and cook on the low setting for 7 hours, until the beef is tender but not shredding.

4. Use a slotted spoon to remove the beef and vegetables from the slow cooker and place them in a large bowl. Strain the liquid through a sieve, reserving the juices and placing any strained vegetables in the bowl with the beef. Discard the bay leaves. Place the beef and vegetables back in the slow cooker. Cover and reduce the heat setting to warm.

5. Melt the remaining 2 tablespoons (28g) of butter in a medium saucepan over medium-low heat. Whisk in the flour. Whisk in the reserved cooking juices. When the mixture comes to a boil, reduce the heat to low. Cook the mixture, whisking constantly, until the sauce thickens, about 10 minutes. Whisk in the horseradish and mustard. Season with salt and pepper to taste.

6. Pour the horseradish sauce over the beef and vegetables in the slow cooker. Re-cover and allow the flavors to marry on the warm setting for at least 1 hour (or up to 3 hours).

7. Stir the sour cream into the stroganoff until the sauce is creamy. Transfer the beef, vegetables, and sauce to a serving bowl and sprinkle with parsley.

Originating in Tsarist Russia in the mid-19th century, beef stroganoff is a popular dish served around the world.

Sweet Pink Banana Butter cuts the spiciness of this dish. Try it with currant jelly or apricot preserves, too.

Spicy Ginger Beef

This spicy-sweet, Indonesian-inspired beef is best served over coconut rice. To make the rice, simply substitute canned coconut milk for half the water in your favorite rice recipe. You can also serve the dish over Persian Rice (see page 158).

Inspiration: Indonesia | **Serves:** 6 to 8 | **Slow cooker time:** 5 hours

INGREDIENTS

- ½ cup (60g) flour
- 1 teaspoon salt
- Black pepper
- 4 pounds (1.8kg) beef stew meat, cut into 1½-inch (4cm) pieces
- 3 tablespoons (45mL) olive oil, divided

- ½ cup (75g) chopped sweet onions, like Vidalia
- 1 dried hot red chili pepper
- ¼ cup (56g) gingerroot paste or grated fresh gingerroot
- 1 tablespoon (14g) plus 1 teaspoon garlic paste or finely minced garlic
- ¼ cup (60mL) fresh lemon juice

- ¼ cup (60mL) honey
- 1 teaspoon Chinese five-spice powder
- 1 tablespoon (1.5g) dried basil
- ⅓ cup (80mL) teriyaki sauce
- ½ cup (120mL) orange juice
- 1 cup (240mL) Pink Banana Butter (see recipe on page 63)

1. Place the flour, salt, and ½ teaspoon (1g) of the black pepper in a large zipper bag. Add about ten pieces of beef to the bag; close it and shake to coat the beef with the flour. Shake the excess flour off each piece and transfer to a large plate. Repeat the process with the remaining beef.

2. Place 1 tablespoon (15mL) of the olive oil in a large nonstick skillet over medium heat. When the oil is hot, place about one-third of the floured beef pieces in the skillet and brown them on all sides, about 1 minute total. Transfer the beef to a 5½-quart (5.2L) slow cooker. Repeat the process with the remaining beef.

3. Add the onions to the skillet and sauté them for about 1 minute, until the onions have softened slightly and absorbed any flour or meat bits. Transfer the onions to the slow cooker. Add the dried chili pepper to the slow cooker.

4. Whisk together the gingerroot paste, garlic, lemon juice, honey, 2 teaspoons (5g) of the black pepper, spice powder, basil, teriyaki sauce, and orange juice in a medium bowl. Pour the mixture over the beef in the slow cooker. Cover the slow cooker and cook for 2 hours. Stir the ingredients and cook for 3 hours more, until the meat is tender but not shredding. Stir in the Pink Banana Butter, reduce the heat setting to warm, and hold for 15 minutes, until the Pink Banana Butter melts. Stir and serve.

Pink Banana Butter

This is not really butter, but banana lovers will savor its sweet flavor and creamy consistency. This is a great recipe for using up overripe bananas.

This sweet treat can also make a great accompaniment to breakfast!

Inspiration: Caribbean | **Makes:** 5 to 6 cups | **Slow cooker time:** 6 to 7 hours

INGREDIENTS

- 4 cups (1L) mashed bananas
- 1 cup (166g) chopped fresh or frozen strawberries
- 1 tablespoon (15mL) melted butter
- ¼ cup (60mL) fresh lime juice

1. Mix the bananas, strawberries, butter, and lime juice together in a 4-quart (3.8L) slow cooker. Cook on the low temperature setting for 6 to 7 hours, until the mixture is pink and smooth.

2. Transfer the mixture to pint canning jars or other covered containers and refrigerate or freeze them until needed.

Everyone has a banana or two that doesn't get eaten in a timely fashion—not rotten but sort of mushy. Don't throw them out! Peel the overripe banana, wrap it in cling film, and freeze it. When you have enough frozen bananas (about seven or eight), simply defrost the bananas, scrape away any darkened parts, mash them, and use them in this recipe.

Picadillo, a classic Cuban comfort food, reaches dinner party status when stuffed into sweet onions.

Picadillo-Stuffed Sweet Onions

Picadillo (pronounced *peek-a-dee-yo*) is one of the most popular dishes in Cuban cuisine. Usually family fare served with fried plantains and black beans, picadillo achieves dinner-party status when stuffed into sweet onions and slow-cooked to perfection. You can prepare the picadillo and stuff the onions a day ahead of time and simply pop them into the slow cooker a few hours before your guests arrive.

Inspiration: Cuba | **Serves:** 4 | **Slow cooker time:** 4 hours

INGREDIENTS

- 4 large sweet onions, like Vidalia, peeled
- 2 teaspoons (10mL) olive oil
- 2 teaspoons (9g) garlic paste or finely minced garlic
- 1 pound (454g) ground beef
- 1 tablespoon (15mL) orange liqueur, optional (I used Grand Marnier)
- ½ cup (75g) raisins
- ⅓ cup (39g) pimento-stuffed green olives, sliced
- 2 tablespoons (15g) capers, rinsed and drained
- ⅓ cup (70g) tomato paste
- ½ teaspoon ground cumin
- ¼ teaspoon dried oregano
- ¾ teaspoon salt
- ¼ teaspoon black pepper
- 1 cup (240mL) beef broth
- 2 tablespoons (28g) butter, melted

1. Slice the stem end off each onion about ½ inch [1.5cm] from the stem. Slice the other end of the onion just enough to remove the root and create a flat edge. Use a serrated melon baller to remove the interior of each onion, leaving the outer two layers intact to form an onion bowl. Place a piece of onion over the hole in the bottom of each onion so the stuffing won't escape. Set the onion bowls aside. Dice the scooped onion, reserving 2 cups (300g) for use in this recipe (place the remaining chopped onions in a zipper bag and refrigerate for future use).

2. Place the oil in a large nonstick skillet over medium heat. Add the diced onions and sauté them, stirring occasionally, for 2½ minutes. Add the garlic and sauté again for 30 seconds. Add the ground beef and cook the mixture, stirring frequently until the meat is browned, about 7 minutes. Drain the beef mixture in a colander. Wipe out the skillet with paper towels and return the meat mixture to the skillet.

3. Place the skillet over medium heat. Add the liqueur, raisins, olives, capers, tomato paste, cumin, oregano, salt, and pepper. Stir to combine the ingredients. Cover the skillet and cook the meat mixture, stirring occasionally, for 7 minutes, until the flavors marry.

4. Place the beef broth in the bottom of a 6-quart (5.7L) slow cooker (or any size that will accommodate the four onions). Brush the interior cavity and outer surface of each onion with melted butter. Spoon the picadillo mixture into each onion, forming a mound on top. Place the onions in the slow cooker. Cover and cook them on the low setting for 4 hours, until the onions have cooked through. (You can hold the stuffed onions on warm setting for up to 30 minutes.)

Moussaka is a textural adventure. The crumbly ground beef balances against tender eggplant, creamy cheese sauce, and a crisp crust on top.

Moussaka

The origin of the word moussaka is believed to be Arabic. Turkey, Lebanon, and other Middle Eastern countries have multiple versions of the dish, but all nations consider this sumptuous layering of eggplant, meat sauce, cheese, and white sauce to be a Greek classic. French-trained Greek chef Nikolaos Tselementes created the modern Greek version of moussaka in the 1920s: all three layers are separately cooked before being assembled for the final baking.

Inspiration: Greece | **Serves:** 4 to 6 | **Slow cooker time:** 3 to 3½ hours

INGREDIENTS

- 2 pounds (907g) graffiti eggplants
- Olive oil spray
- 1 pound (454g) ground beef
- 1 cup (150g) chopped sweet onions, like Vidalia
- 1 teaspoon garlic paste or finely minced garlic

- One 8-ounce (227g) can tomato sauce
- One 1.37-ounce (38g) envelope dry tomato sauce mix (I used McCormick Thick & Zesty Spaghetti Sauce Mix)
- ¾ cup (180mL) red wine
- ⅓ cup (20g) fresh breadcrumbs

- One 8-ounce (227g) package shredded Monterey Jack cheese, divided
- 1 tablespoon (14g) butter
- 1 tablespoon (7.5g) flour
- 1 cup (252g) evaporated milk

1. Preheat the oven to 250°F (130°C). Cut off the top and bottom and peel each eggplant. Cut the eggplants into ¼-inch-wide (6.5mm-wide) slices. Place the eggplant slices on baking sheets and coat them liberally with olive oil spray. Bake them for 10 minutes. Turn the slices over and coat them liberally with olive oil spray. Bake them for 10 minutes more. Remove the eggplant slices from the oven and divide them equally among three small plates. Set them aside.

2. Place the ground beef in a large nonstick skillet over medium heat. Sauté the meat until it's browned, stirring occasionally, about 3 to 4 minutes. Drain the browned beef in a colander and return it to the skillet. Add the onions and garlic and sauté the mixture for 1 minute, stirring constantly.

3. Stir in the tomato sauce, tomato sauce dry mix, and wine. Reduce the heat to low and simmer the mixture for 5 minutes, stirring occasionally. Remove it from the heat and set it aside.

4. Sprinkle the breadcrumbs in the bottom of a 4-quart (3.8L) slow cooker. Place one-third of the eggplant slices in a layer on top of the crumbs. Spread one-half of the meat mixture over the eggplant. Sprinkle ½ cup (56g) of the shredded cheese on top of the meat mixture. Repeat the layers: one-third of the eggplant slices, one-half of the meat mixture, ½ cup (56g) of the shredded cheese. Place the final one-third of the eggplant slices in a layer on top of the cheese.

5. Melt the butter in a small nonstick saucepan over medium-low heat. Whisk in the flour to form a roux. Whisk in the evaporated milk and continue whisking until the mixture just comes to a boil, about 1 minute. Remove the saucepan from the heat and whisk in the remaining cheese (about 1 cup [112g]). Pour the cheese sauce over the eggplant in the slow cooker.

6. Cover the slow cooker and cook everything on the low setting for 3 to 3½ hours, until the filling is firm and the cheese sauce is crusty on top.

7. Cut the moussaka into wedges and serve.

Graffiti eggplants are ivory with purple markings or purple with ivory markings. They are smooth and creamy when cooked and aren't as bitter as large purple-black eggplants tend to be. If you can't find them in your supermarket, substitute small, smooth-skinned purple-black eggplants, which will taste milder than their larger cousins.

Tomatoes, green olives, and soppressata marry in a savory sauce that swaddles the Catalan meatballs.

Catalan Meatballs (*Boules de Picolat*) with Green Olive Sauce

A specialty of the Roussillon area of southeastern France, which has a heavy Spanish influence from its shared border of the Pyrenees, these beef and sausage meatballs are swaddled in a savory sauce of tomatoes, olives, and *soppressata* (Italian slow-aged, dried salami). Locals eat the sauce-topped meatballs with cooked white beans, but new red or white potatoes are wonderful, as well.

Inspiration: France | **Serves:** 4 to 6 | **Slow cooker time:** 4 hours

INGREDIENTS

- 8 ounces (227g) lean ground beef
- 1 pound (454g) sweet Italian pork sausage, casings removed
- 5 teaspoons garlic paste or finely minced garlic
- 2 tablespoons (8g) snipped flat-leaf parsley
- 1 pinch dried thyme
- Salt and freshly ground black pepper
- 2 eggs, beaten
- ¼ cup (30g) flour
- 2 tablespoons (30mL) olive oil, divided
- 1½ cups (225g) chopped sweet onions, like Vidalia
- One 14.5-ounce (411g) can petite-diced tomatoes with juices
- 2 ounces (57g) soppressata or prosciutto, cut into a small dice
- ¼ teaspoon crushed red pepper flakes
- ⅛ teaspoon ground cinnamon
- ½ teaspoon paprika
- ¾ cup (135g) pitted green olives without pimento

1. Crumble the ground beef and sausage into a large bowl. Add the garlic, parsley, thyme, salt, and pepper to taste. Mix the ingredients together with clean hands. Add the eggs and mix the ingredients together well.

2. Place the flour on a dinner plate. Form the meat mixture into golf ball–size meatballs and roll each in flour. Set them on a clean plate. (The meatballs will adhere together loosely.) Repeat with the remaining meat mixture.

3. Place 1 tablespoon (15mL) of the oil in a large nonstick skillet over medium heat. Add half the meatballs and sauté them, turning the meatballs frequently until they are browned, about 4 minutes. Transfer the meatballs to a 4-quart (3.8L) slow cooker. Repeat the process with the remaining oil and meatballs.

4. Add the onions to the skillet and sauté them for 2 minutes. Stir in the tomatoes, soppressata, red pepper flakes, cinnamon, paprika, and 1½ cups (360mL) of water. Bring the mixture to a boil over medium heat. Reduce the heat to medium-low and simmer for 5 minutes.

5. Sprinkle the olives over the meatballs in the slow cooker. Pour the sauce over the meatballs. Cover the slow cooker and cook on the low setting for 4 hours. Serve immediately.

> *Yellow, red, and orange peppers are sweeter than green peppers, which are not yet ripe. Chop up the tops of your peppers and reserve them for use in a tossed salad.*

Persian Stuffed Bell Peppers

Just about every cuisine in the world has a version of stuffed bell peppers. Some stuff eggplants, zucchini, tomatoes, onions, and even potatoes, with a savory mixture of rice, meat, onions, herbs, spices, and sometimes dried fruits or nuts. This recipe spotlights the seasonings of ancient Persia, which used copious amounts of parsley and mint, as well as a concoction of spices known as *advieh* (see the sidebar on page 71).

Inspiration: Iran | **Serves:** 4 (two peppers per person) | **Slow cooker time:** 5 to 6 hours

INGREDIENTS

- ¼ cup (55g) basmati or long-grain rice
- ¼ cup (56g) yellow split peas
- 8 red, yellow, or orange bell peppers
- 1 tablespoon (15mL) olive oil
- 1 cup (150g) chopped sweet onions, like Vidalia
- 1 pound (454g) ground beef
- 2 tablespoons (28g) tomato paste

- 1 cup (25g) snipped fresh flat-leaf parsley
- ½ cup (15g) snipped fresh mint
- ½ cup (52g) minced scallions
- 1 teaspoon dried tarragon
- 2¼ teaspoons salt, divided
- ½ teaspoon black pepper
- ¼ teaspoon advieh (see the sidebar on page 71)

- Vegetable cooking spray
- 1½ cups (360mL) tomato juice
- ¼ cup (50g) light brown sugar
- 1 tablespoon (15mL) fresh lemon juice
- 2 tablespoons (29g) Parmesan cheese

1. Place the rice and split peas in a medium bowl. Add water to cover them and agitate the mixture with your hand. Drain off the water. Repeat the process two more times to remove excess starch from the rice. Drain the mixture in a colander. Place the rinsed rice and peas and 2 cups (480mL) of water in a medium saucepan over high heat. Bring everything to a boil, stir the mixture, and reduce the heat to medium. Cook for 15 minutes, stirring occasionally. Transfer the mixture to a colander. Rinse it and drain.

2. Meanwhile, cut the tops off the bell peppers. Remove the seeds and ribs from the interior of the peppers. Rinse and drain them on paper towels.

3. Place the olive oil in a large nonstick skillet over medium heat. Add the onions and ground beef and cook the mixture, stirring frequently, until the meat is browned, about 5 minutes. Stir in the tomato paste. Remove from the heat and stir in the rice and split peas.

4. Transfer the meat mixture to a large bowl. Add the parsley, mint, scallions, tarragon, 1 teaspoon (6g) of the salt, black pepper, and advieh. Toss until the ingredients are well combined.

5. Coat the interior of a 6-quart (5.7L) slow cooker with vegetable cooking spray. Fill each bell pepper with the meat stuffing and place them in the slow cooker.

6. Whisk the tomato juice, brown sugar, lemon juice, and ¼ teaspoon (1.5g) of the salt together in a measuring cup. Pour the liquid around the stuffed peppers in the slow cooker, taking care not to pour the liquid into the stuffing.

7. Cover the slow cooker and cook on the low setting for 5 to 6 hours, until the peppers are soft.

8. Remove the peppers to a serving platter. Sprinkle each with Parmesan cheese. Drizzle the sauce over the peppers. Serve immediately.

Advieh

Advieh is a Persian rice seasoning composed of many spices. Advieh simply means "spice" in Farsi. You can find it in Middle Eastern markets or online at vendors such as *www.sadaf.com*. To make a reasonable facsimile on your own, mix together 1 teaspoon ground cinnamon, 1 teaspoon ground nutmeg, 1 teaspoon ground cardamom, and ½ teaspoon ground cumin. Store the mixture in an airtight container.

Authentic advieh also contains ground rose petals, which are not readily found in American supermarkets, but can be purchased online. Add 1 teaspoon to your advieh mixture. (The seasoning mix will taste fine without the additional of ground rose petals.)

Currant-Glazed Corned Beef

Referred to as "boiled beef dinner" in England, corned beef is a staple meal all around the United Kingdom. Before the days of refrigeration, beef was cured in salt brine for preservation. The term "corned" refers to the corns, or grains, of salt in which it is cured.

Inspiration: Great Britain | **Serves:** 6 to 8 | **Slow cooker time:** 6½ hours

INGREDIENTS

- 3¾ to 4 pounds (1.7 to 1.8kg) flat-cut corned beef brisket
- 2 tablespoons (3g) snipped fresh mint
- 3 tablespoons (37.5g) brown sugar
- 1½ tablespoons (23mL) cider vinegar
- ¼ cup (60mL) plus 1 tablespoon (15mL) orange juice, divided
- 2 dried red hot peppers
- 4 whole cloves
- 8 thin sweet onion slices, like Vidalia
- 4 peeled white sweet potatoes, cut into 1½-inch (4cm) chunks
- 2 cups (300g) baby carrots
- ½ cup (120mL) heavy whipping cream
- 3 tablespoons (45mL) prepared horseradish
- ⅓ cup (80mL) red currant jelly
- ½ tablespoon (8mL) orange liqueur (I used Grand Marnier)

1. Rinse the corned beef and dry it with paper towels. Place it in a 5½-quart (5.2L) stovetop-proof slow cooker, fat side down, and brown for 2 minutes. Turn the corned beef and brown the other side for 2 minutes. Remove it from the heat and sprinkle the mint atop the corned beef.

2. Whisk together the brown sugar, vinegar, and ¼ cup (60mL) of the orange juice. Pour the mixture over the corned beef. Add the peppers and cloves to the slow cooker on either side of the corned beef. Place the onions over the corned beef like a blanket. Add water to just cover corned beef. Cover the slow cooker and cook on the low setting for 5½ hours. Add the sweet potatoes and carrots to the slow cooker, immersing them in the liquid. Re-cover and cook for 1 more hour, until the carrots and potatoes are fork-tender.

3. Meanwhile, whip the cream until soft peaks form. Fold in the horseradish. Refrigerate the mixture until needed.

4. Just before serving, place the jelly, 1 tablespoon (15mL) of the orange juice, and the orange liqueur in a small saucepan over medium-low heat. Stirring constantly, cook until the jelly has melted, about 1 minute.

5. Transfer the corned beef to a serving platter using two firm spatulas. Drizzle the jelly glaze over the corned beef. Cut the corned beef into slices. Use a slotted spoon to remove the vegetables from the slow cooker and place them in a circle around the corned beef. Serve immediately with the horseradish cream on the side.

White sweet potatoes can be found in the autumn farmers' markets in many areas of the country. If you can't find them, substitute small, white new potatoes instead.

The horseradish cream adds a tangy counterpoint to the sweet currant glaze on the corned beef.

This recipe approximates a dish I enjoyed when I visited Cape Town.

Cape Malay Lamb Curry

In the seventeenth century, Indonesians were brought to Cape Town, South Africa, to be enslaved labor on the farms of the western Cape. Known as Cape Malays, they carried with them a spicy-sweet cuisine that has become an enduring favorite in the region and beyond. Serve the curry with steamed white rice.

Inspiration: South Africa | **Serves:** 4 to 6 | **Slow cooker time:** 4½ to 5½ hours

INGREDIENTS

- 3 tablespoons (45mL) olive oil, divided
- 6 cups (600g) halved and thinly sliced sweet onions, like Vidalia
- 1 tablespoon (14g) garlic paste or finely minced garlic
- 2 pounds (907g) boneless leg of lamb, cleaned of all fat and cut into 1½-inch (4cm) pieces
- ¾ teaspoon salt, divided
- 1 tablespoon (14g) Thai red curry paste
- 2 teaspoons Gourmet Garden Thai seasoning paste
- 1 teaspoon gingerroot paste or peeled and grated gingerroot
- ½ teaspoon turmeric
- ¼ cup (60mL) lemon juice
- 1 tablespoon (15mL) tamarind syrup
- 2 tablespoons (30mL) sweetened cream of coconut (I used Coco López)
- 1 cup (240mL) water

1. Place 2 tablespoons (30mL) of the oil in a large nonstick skillet over medium heat. Add the onions and sauté them, stirring frequently, for 4 minutes. Add the garlic and cook the mixture for 4 minutes more, stirring frequently. Transfer the mixture to a 4-quart (3.8L) slow cooker.

2. Add 1 tablespoon (15mL) of the oil to the skillet. Sprinkle the lamb with salt. Add half the lamb pieces to the skillet and brown them over medium heat, about 2 minutes. Use a slotted spoon to place the lamb in the slow cooker. Repeat the browning process with the remaining lamb pieces and place them in the slow cooker.

3. Place the curry paste, seasoning paste, gingerroot, turmeric, lemon juice, tamarind syrup, salt, cream of coconut, and water in a medium bowl. Whisk the ingredients into a smooth sauce. Pour the sauce into the slow cooker. Stir to combine all the ingredients.

4. Cover the slow cooker and cook on the low setting for 4½ to 5½ hours, until the lamb is fork-tender. Serve Immediately.

Thai red curry paste is made from ground red hot chili peppers. Tamarind syrup, made from the fruit of the tamarind tree, is like the lemon juice of Indonesia. You can find both ingredients in the international section of your supermarket. Coco López is a thick, sweetened coconut cream, often used in tropical drinks. You can find it in the beverage section of your supermarket.

Lamb in Peanut-Chili Sauce

This Southeast Asian–inspired sauced lamb calls for spicy brown bean sauce, which is a robust sauce made from fermented soybeans, sugar, sherry, garlic, and other spices. It, along with fish sauce—a salty sauce essential to much of the cuisine of the region—can be found in the international section of your supermarket. Serve it with coconut rice. (To make coconut rice, simply replace half the water needed to cook your favorite rice with coconut milk.)

Inspiration: Southeast Asia | **Serves:** 4 | **Slow cooker time:** 5 hours

INGREDIENTS

- ¼ cup (37g) unsalted, dry-roasted peanuts
- 1½ tablespoons (13g) sesame seeds
- 1 tablespoon (15mL) canola oil
- 1 tablespoon (14g) garlic paste or finely minced garlic
- ¼ cup (60mL) spicy brown bean sauce
- 1 tablespoon (14g) tomato paste
- 1 tablespoon (15mL) fish sauce
- 1 tablespoon (16g) peanut butter
- 1 cup (240mL) warm water
- 1 tablespoon (12g) sugar
- ½ cup (60g) flour
- 1¾ pounds (794g) boneless leg of lamb, cut into 1-inch (2.5cm) pieces
- 2 tablespoons (30mL) olive oil

1. Up to one week ahead, dry-toast the peanuts in a small nonstick skillet over medium heat for about 3 minutes, or until they are fragrant and browned slightly. Transfer them to a food processor and pulse until the peanuts are finely chopped. Set them aside.

2. Place the sesame seeds in a skillet and dry-toast them for 1 to 2 minutes, stirring constantly, until the seeds have browned slightly. Remove the skillet from the heat and set it aside.

3. Place the oil in a medium nonstick saucepan over medium-low heat. When the oil is hot, add the garlic, bean sauce, tomato paste, and fish sauce and stir to combine. Whisk together the peanut butter, water, and sugar in a small bowl until smooth. Whisk the peanut butter liquid into the sauce mixture in the saucepan.

4. Increase the heat to medium-high and bring the sauce to a boil, stirring constantly. Reduce the heat to low and simmer for 2 minutes, stirring occasionally. Remove from the heat and set it aside or place it in a covered container and refrigerate until needed. (If refrigerated, reheat the sauce in a nonstick saucepan on low before proceeding with the remaining steps.)

5. Place the flour in a large zipper bag. Add the lamb pieces in batches, shaking until the pieces are coated with flour. Shake off any excess flour and place the pieces on a dinner plate.

6. Place the oil in a large nonstick skillet over medium heat. When the oil is hot, add half the lamb pieces and sauté them until browned on all sides, about 1 to 2 minutes. Use a slotted spoon to transfer the lamb to a 1½- or 2-quart (1.4 or 1.9L) slow cooker. Repeat with the remaining lamb pieces. Sprinkle the ground peanuts and dry-roasted sesame seeds over the lamb in the slow cooker.

7. Pour the peanut-chili sauce over the lamb, poking any exposed lamb pieces down into the sauce. Cover the slow cooker and cook on the low setting for 5 hours, until the lamb is fork-tender.

I first encountered this robust sauce in Singapore many years ago. I was hooked!

The succulent lamb falls off the bone and melts in your mouth.

Braised Lamb Shanks

Trimming every bit of fat from the lamb shanks is a laborious task, but the end result is worth every minute of effort. After hours of braising in this lemon-tomato-mint sauce, the meat is tender and flavorful. Serve the lamb with Persian Rice (see recipe on page 158).

Inspiration: Mediterranean Rim | **Serves:** 4 | **Slow cooker time:** 7½ hours

INGREDIENTS

- 3 large lamb shanks (about 3 pounds [1.5kg])
- 2 tablespoons (30mL) olive oil, divided
- 3 cups (450g) chopped onions
- 2 teaspoons garlic paste or finely minced garlic
- 1 teaspoon salt
- ½ teaspoon black pepper
- 1 teaspoon turmeric
- One 8-ounce (227g) can tomato sauce
- 6 tablespoons (90mL) fresh lemon juice
- ½ cup (15g) snipped fresh mint
- 3 granny smith apples, peeled, cored, and sliced

1. Trim all the fat from the lamb shanks and discard it. Place 1 tablespoon (5mL) of the oil in a large nonstick skillet over medium heat. When the oil is hot, add the lamb shanks and sear them until browned, about 3 minutes. Transfer the shanks to a 5- to 5½-quart (4.8 to 5.2L) slow cooker.

2. Add the remaining 1 tablespoon (15mL) of oil to skillet. Add the onions, garlic, salt, pepper, and turmeric. Sauté the onions over medium heat, stirring frequently, until they are a dark golden color, about 5 minutes. Stir in the tomato sauce, lemon juice, and mint. Pour the onion mixture over the lamb shanks in the slow cooker.

3. Cover the slow cooker and cook on the low setting for 6 hours. Place the apple slices atop the lamb mixture. Re-cover the slow cooker and cook for 1½ hours more, until the lamb has fallen off the bone and the apples have cooked down. Remove the shank bones, stir, and serve immediately or hold on the warm setting for up to 1 hour.

You'll have about 1 pound (454g) of fat from the trimmed lamb shanks. Once the bones are discarded, you'll end up with slightly less than 1 pound (454g) of actual meat. To serve six people, you can add another lamb shank or two without having to increase the sauce proportions.

The tagine stands alone as an entrée, but you can serve it with a side of couscous or rice if you'd like.

Moroccan Lamb Tagine

Your taste buds will be transported to Marrakesh with this savory lamb stew ubiquitous in the region. Tagine, a slow-cooked stew that is braised at low temperatures, is named after the heavy clay pot in which it is cooked in North Africa (see Tagine Clay Pot Cooking on page 81). Don't let the long ingredient list put you off—the spice rub and overnight marinating of the lamb accounts for nearly half. It's great to have these spices in your kitchen stash, but if you are missing one or two of the ingredients, the stew will still be flavorful.

Inspiration: Morocco and North Africa | **Serves:** 4 | **Slow cooker time:** 4 to 4½ hours

INGREDIENTS

- 1 teaspoon coarse salt
- ¼ teaspoon cayenne pepper
- ¾ teaspoon garlic powder
- 2 teaspoons paprika
- ¼ teaspoon turmeric
- ½ teaspoon ground cumin
- 1 teaspoon ground cinnamon
- ¾ teaspoon ground coriander
- ½ teaspoon ground ginger
- ¼ teaspoon ground cloves
- ½ teaspoon ground cardamom
- 2 teaspoons dried mint leaves

- 1¾ to 2 pounds (794 to 907g) boneless leg of lamb, cut into 1-inch (2.5cm) pieces
- ¼ cup (60mL) olive oil, divided
- 3 cups (450g) roughly chopped sweet onions, like Vidalia
- 3 cups (420g) peeled, seeded butternut squash chunks (1-inch [2.5cm] pieces)
- 4 teaspoons garlic paste or finely minced garlic
- 1 tablespoon (14g) gingerroot paste or finely minced gingerroot

- 1 lemon
- 1½ tablespoons (23mL) honey
- One 14.5-ounce (411g) can petite-diced tomatoes, drained, rinsed, and drained again
- One 19-ounce (569g) can chickpeas, drained
- ¾ cup (115g) pitted prunes
- ¾ cup (98g) dried apricots
- ¾ cup (180mL) chicken broth
- ¼ cup (60mL) orange juice
- Mint sauce (bottled)

1. One day ahead, mix the salt, cayenne pepper, garlic powder, paprika, turmeric, cumin, cinnamon, coriander, ginger, cloves, cardamom, and mint leaves together in a small bowl. Place the lamb in a large freezer-weight zipper bag. Add the spice mixture and close the bag. Shake the bag until the lamb pieces are well coated with spices. Add 2 tablespoons (30mL) of the olive oil to the bag. Close the bag and manipulate the lamb pieces until they are coated with the oil, herbs, and spices. Refrigerate until needed.

2. Place 1 tablespoon (15mL) of the oil in a large nonstick skillet over medium heat. Add the lamb pieces and sauté them until browned, about 3 to 4 minutes. Transfer to a 5- to 5½-quart (4.8 to 5.2L) slow cooker. Add the remaining 1 tablespoon (15mL) of oil to the skillet. Add the onions and squash, and sauté for 3 minutes. Add the garlic and gingerroot pastes and sauté for 3 minutes more. Transfer the vegetable mixture to the slow cooker.

3. Grate the lemon peel with a zester. Squeeze the juice from the lemon. Add the juice and lemon peel to the slow cooker. Add the honey, tomatoes, chickpeas, prunes, apricots, broth, and orange juice to the slow cooker. Stir until the ingredients are well combined.

4. Cover the slow cooker and cook on the low setting for 4 to 4½ hours, until the lamb is tender and the squash is cooked through. Serve each portion in a large shallow soup bowl. Lace the tagine with mint sauce to taste. (You can hold the tagine for up to 1 hour on the warm setting.)

Tagine Clay Pot Cooking

Dating back centuries, the tagine has long been the cooking vessel of choice throughout the Middle East and North Africa. Like an ancient version of the modern slow cooker, the distinctively shaped natural clay pot slowly cooks ingredients, deeply infusing them with the sweet and spicy flavors of the herbs and spices used. Tagines are used to make North African stews of the same name—tagines.

The tagine's conical shape creates a uniquely moist, hot environment for cooking the ingredients. Its base is wide and shallow. The tall, conical lid fits snugly inside. As the food cooks, steam from it rises into the cone, condenses, then drips down the sides and back into the dish. Traditionally the tagine was placed over a smoldering charcoal fire, where the fire's smoke permeated it. Today, tagines are commonly glazed, which makes cleaning them easier (food doesn't stick to the bottom as it often does on an unglazed raw clay vessel). Serving-only tagines are also popular for presenting side dishes, although they cannot touch a heat source. They range in size from 1 quart (946mL) to 4 quarts (3.8L).

Stuffed Grape Leaves with Lemon Sauce

Nearly every country in the Mediterranean Rim and Eastern Europe serves a variation of stuffed grape leaves. All belonging to the family of "dolma" (a word of Turkish origin meaning stuffed or filled), they are usually stuffed with meat or grain fillings and served with a garlic-yogurt sauce or a sweet-and-sour pomegranate sauce. Called *dolmeh* in Iran, *tolma* in Armenia, or *yebra* in Syria, this Greek version, called *dolmades*, encapsulates a savory mixture of ground lamb, rice, and mint in the ubiquitous grape leaves.

Inspiration: Greece | **Serves:** 8 | **Slow cooker time:** 4 to 4½ hours

INGREDIENTS

- 1 tablespoon (15mL) olive oil
- 2 cups (300g) chopped sweet onions, like Vidalia
- 2 teaspoons salt, divided
- 1 pound (454g) ground lamb
- ½ cup (115g) uncooked jasmine or other long-grained rice
- ¼ teaspoon black pepper
- 2 tablespoons (3g) snipped fresh mint
- One 15.2-ounce (431g) jar grapevine leaves
- ¾ cup (180mL) dry white wine
- ¾ cup (180mL) chicken broth
- ¼ cup (60mL) fresh lemon juice
- 2 teaspoons cornstarch
- 1½ teaspoons sugar
- 2 tablespoons (28g) butter

1. Place the oil in a large nonstick skillet over medium heat. Add the onions and 1 teaspoon (4g) of the salt. Sauté the onions until they are soft but not brown, about 4 minutes, stirring occasionally. Transfer half the onions to a large bowl.

2. Add the lamb, rice, pepper, 1 teaspoon (4g) of the salt, and mint to the bowl. Mix the ingredients together with clean hands.

3. Rinse the grape leaves and drain them on paper towels. Carefully separate the leaves. Place a double layer of leaves on a clean work surface. Place a rounded spoonful of the lamb mixture in the middle of each leaf. Fold the stem ends over the filling, then fold in the sides and roll the leaves up tightly. Place the rolled leaves, seam side down, in the bottom of a 2-quart (1.9L) slow cooker. Repeat the process with the remaining leaves and meat filling, creating two layers of stuffed, rolled leaves.

4. Sprinkle the remaining onions over the rolled grape leaves. Pour 1½ cups (360mL) water over the contents of the slow cooker. Cover the slow cooker and cook on the low setting for 4 to 4½ hours, until the rice and lamb are cooked through and the leaves are tender.

5. About 30 minutes before serving, make the lemon sauce. Place the wine and broth in a 2-quart (1.9L) nonstick saucepan over medium-high heat. Bring it to a boil and cook for about 8 minutes, stirring frequently, until the mixture reduces by half. Whisk together the lemon juice, cornstarch, and sugar in a small bowl and slowly stir it into the broth mixture. Keep stirring until the sauce boils again. Stir in the butter. Reduce the heat to low, cover the saucepan, and keep the sauce warm.

6. Once ready, use a slotted spoon to transfer the stuffed grape leaves to a serving platter. Drizzle them with the lemon sauce. Serve the remaining sauce on the side.

You'll find jarred grape leaves in the
international section of your supermarket
or in specialty grocery stores.

The lemon-egg sauce, a cousin to Greek avgolemono sauce, bathes the succulent lamb pieces.

Lemon-Artichoke Veal Stew

French chefs hired by Italian nobles devised this tasty stew, which combines the artichokes of Sicily and the lemons of Ravello. Artichokes are a type of thistle. They are widely cultivated throughout Italy, which grows almost 1 billion pounds (454 million kg) of artichokes a year.

Inspiration: Italy | **Serves:** 6 | **Slow cooker time:** 5 to 5½ hours

INGREDIENTS

- ½ cup (60g) flour
- 1¼ teaspoons salt, divided
- ½ teaspoon black pepper, divided
- 3 pounds (1.5kg) veal stew meat, cut into 2- to 2½-inch (5 to 6.5cm) cubes
- 6 tablespoons (90mL) olive oil, divided
- 1 cup (150g) chopped sweet onions, like Vidalia
- 4 teaspoons garlic paste or finely minced garlic
- ½ teaspoon crushed red pepper flakes
- 4 teaspoons freshly grated lemon peel
- One 13.75-ounce (390g) can whole artichoke hearts, rinsed, drained, and quartered
- 6 tablespoons (90mL) white wine
- 1½ cups (360mL) chicken broth
- ¼ cup (60mL) fresh lemon juice
- 2 large eggs
- ½ cup (13g) snipped fresh flat-leaf parsley, divided
- 1 pound (454g) wide egg noodles

1. Place the flour, ½ teaspoon of the salt, and ¼ teaspoon of the pepper in a large zipper bag. Add the veal to the bag, about five pieces at a time. Shake the bag so the flour coats the veal. Shake off any excess flour and transfer the flour-dusted veal to a large plate.

2. Place 2 tablespoons (30mL) of the oil in a large nonstick skillet over medium heat. When the oil is hot, add about one-third of the veal cubes. Brown the veal for about 30 seconds per side. Transfer the veal to a 4-quart (3.8L) slow cooker. Repeat the browning process two more times, adding 2 tablespoons (30mL) of oil each time and transferring the browned veal to the slow cooker.

3. Add the onions, garlic, crushed red pepper, lemon peel, ½ teaspoon of the salt, ¼ teaspoon of the pepper, and artichokes to the skillet. Sauté the mixture, stirring constantly, for 1 minute. Add the wine and sauté, stirring constantly for 1 minute. Add the broth and lemon juice and bring to a boil, about 1 minute. Pour the mixture over the veal in the slow cooker. Stir the ingredients.

4. Cover the slow cooker and cook on the low setting for 4½ to 5 hours. Use a slotted spoon to remove the veal and artichokes to a large bowl. Cover the bowl with aluminum foil. Whisk the eggs, ½ teaspoon of the salt, and ¼ cup (7g) of the parsley together until frothy. Whisk the egg mixture into the liquid remaining in the slow cooker. Cover the slow cooker and cook the sauce on high for 10 minutes. Transfer the veal and artichokes back to the slow cooker. Stir to combine the ingredients. Cover the slow cooker and cook on high for 10 minutes more.

5. Meanwhile, bring a large pot of water to boil over medium-high heat. Cook the egg noodles according to the package directions until they're al dente. Drain the noodles in a colander.

6. Divide the noodles among six large pasta bowls or dinner plates. Top each with equal portions of veal stew and sauce. Sprinkle each serving with the remaining parsley and serve.

Pura Ulun Danu Bratan is a major Hindu temple in Bali, Indonesia.

POULTRY AND PORK

Poultry and pork are the most versatile of meats, partnering
seamlessly with a wide range of international ingredients.

VEGETARIAN ITEMS

Fruited Chicken

Called *manchamanteles* or "tablecloth stainers" in Mexico, this traditional fruit-laden stew is spiked with cinnamon and chili powder. Serve with steamed white rice or Persian Rice (see the recipe on page 158) and lots of corn tortillas to sop up the sauce.

Inspiration: Mexico | **Serves:** 8 | **Slow cooker time:** 4½ hours

INGREDIENTS

- 2 tablespoons (30mL) olive oil
- 4½ pounds (2kg) skinless, boneless chicken thighs, trimmed of excess fat
- 1 cup (150g) chopped sweet onions, like Vidalia
- 1 cup (175g) diced green bell peppers
- ¼ cup (27g) slivered almonds
- ½ cup (121g) crushed tomatoes or tomato puree
- One 15-ounce (425g) can mandarin orange segments, drained with juices reserved
- 2 teaspoons chili powder
- 1 teaspoon salt
- ½ teaspoon ground cinnamon
- 1 tablespoon Mexican herb and spice blend
- 2 sweet-tart apples, peeled, cored, and sliced
- 2 bananas, peeled and sliced into ½-inch (1.5cm) pieces
- 2 tablespoons (24g) cornstarch

1. Place the oil in a large nonstick skillet over medium heat. Working in two batches, brown the chicken on both sides, about 1 minute total. Transfer to a 5- or 6-quart (4.8 to 5.7L) slow cooker. Add the onions, bell peppers, and almonds to the skillet. Sauté until the vegetables are browned slightly, about 3 minutes.

2. Transfer the vegetables to a blender. Add the crushed tomatoes or tomato puree, ½ cup (120mL) of the reserved mandarin orange juice, chili powder, salt, cinnamon, and Mexican spice blend. Puree the mixture until smooth.

3. Pour the mixture over the chicken in the slow cooker. Cover the slow cooker and cook on the low setting for 3 hours. Add the apples, bananas, and mandarin oranges. Re-cover the slow cooker and cook for 1½ hours more, until the apples have cooked through but are not mushy.

4. Use a slotted spoon to remove the chicken and fruit, placing it in a low-sided serving dish with the fruit on top of the chicken. Cover the dish with aluminum foil.

5. Place the cornstarch in a medium bowl. Whisk in 1 cup (240mL) of the sauce from the slow cooker until smooth. Whisk the cornstarch mixture into the slow cooker. Cover the slow cooker and cook on the high setting for 5 to 10 minutes, whisking occasionally, until the sauce has thickened. Pour the sauce over the fruit and chicken and serve immediately.

Manchamanteles is considered to be a type of mole sauce.

The blanket of sliced tomatoes keeps the chicken breasts moist. You can remove them before serving if desired.

Herbed Chicken Dijon

Chicken Dijon is a classic, traditional French dish. As the story goes, the wife of the mayor of Dijon was making dinner for a famous gastronomic critic when a container of mustard accidentally fell into the pan. Copious amounts of mustard spread over the chicken pieces as they cooked. Frantically trying to salvage her dish, she smothered it even more with white wine and sour cream. It is no accident that this version of Chicken Dijon is considerably lighter!

Inspiration: France | **Serves:** 4 | **Slow cooker time:** 4 hours

INGREDIENTS

- ½ cup (60g) flour
- 4 large skinless, boneless chicken breasts, cut in half
- 2 tablespoons (30mL) olive oil
- 2 teaspoons garlic paste or minced garlic
- 1 tablespoon (14g) gingerroot paste or peeled, minced gingerroot
- 1 tablespoon (15mL) Dijon mustard
- 1 teaspoon salt
- 1 teaspoon freshly ground black pepper
- 2 large plum tomatoes (about 9 ounces [255g]), thinly sliced
- 1 teaspoon snipped fresh flat-leafed parsley
- 1 teaspoon snipped fresh rosemary
- ¼ cup (15g) fresh breadcrumbs
- 1 tablespoon (14g) butter, melted

1. Place the flour in a large zipper bag. Add half the chicken pieces to the bag. Close and shake the bag until the chicken is coated with flour. Shake off any excess flour and transfer the chicken to a dinner plate. Repeat with the remaining chicken.

2. Place the oil in a large nonstick skillet over medium heat. When the oil is hot, add the chicken and sear it for about 30 seconds per side. Transfer the chicken to a 2-quart (1.9L) slow cooker in a single, tight layer.

3. Mix the gingerroot, garlic, and mustard together in a small bowl. Spread the mustard paste over the chicken. Sprinkle with the salt and pepper. Place the tomato slices in an even layer atop the chicken. Sprinkle with the parsley, rosemary, and breadcrumbs. Drizzle the melted butter over the breadcrumbs. Cover the slow cooker and cook on the low setting for 4 hours, until the chicken is no longer pink when tested with a knife. (The chicken should just be cooked through and still moist.)

4. Remove each chicken breast from the slow cooker and place them on a serving platter. Drizzle the chicken with cooking juices.

Dijon Mustard

Dijon, in the Burgundy region of France, was the center of French mustard making in the Middle Ages. Dijon mustard assumed its current form in 1856 when Jean Naigeon changed the recipe, substituting the plain vinegar previously used with verjuice, the acidic juice from unripe grapes. The modern Dijon-style mustard is made up of brown mustard seeds and a combination of white wine, vinegar, water, and salt that imitates the flavor of Naigeon's verjuice addition.

West African Chicken and Peanut Stew

Peanut stew is a staple of African cuisine. My two trips to Africa revealed unexpectedly complex flavors concocted from ingredients that can also be commonly found in the United States, such as sweet potatoes, hot chilis, and peanuts. I found that these groundnut stews combine the West African holy trinity of groundnuts, onions, and chilis with a protein component, often chicken.

Inspiration: West Africa | **Serves:** 6 | **Slow cooker time:** 4 hours

INGREDIENTS

- 2 pounds (907g) skinless, boneless chicken breasts, cut into 1½-inch (4cm) chunks
- Salt and freshly ground black pepper
- 1 cup (150g) chopped sweet onions, like Vidalia

- 2 large sweet potatoes, peeled, sliced 1¼-inch (3cm) thick, and slices quartered
- 2 to 3 fresh serrano chilies, thinly sliced (see the tip box below)
- 3 large tomatoes, peeled and cut into a large dice

- ½ teaspoon coarse salt
- ½ teaspoon sugar
- ½ cup (125g) chunky peanut butter
- ½ cup (120mL) hot water
- 1 tablespoon (14g) garlic paste or finely minced garlic
- ½ cup (120mL) red currant jelly

1. Liberally season the chicken with salt and pepper. Place the chicken in a 5-quart (4.8-L) slow cooker. Add the onions, sweet potatoes, chilies, and tomatoes. Stir so that ingredients are well mixed. Sprinkle the ingredients with coarse salt and sugar.

2. Place the peanut butter in a medium bowl. Whisk in the water and garlic paste. Pour the mixture over the ingredients in the slow cooker. Cook on the low setting for 5 hours. Stir in the red currant jelly. Re-cover and cook for 30 minutes more on the low setting or reduce the heat to warm and hold for 1 hour. Serve in large, shallow soup bowls.

I used three serrano chilies in this recipe, which makes the dish very spicy. If you prefer less heat, use only one or two chilies.

To easily peel your tomatoes, bring a medium saucepan of water to a boil over high heat. Cut an X on the tops and the stem ends of the tomatoes. Add the tomatoes to the boiling water, one at a time, leaving them in the water for only about 15 seconds. Use tongs to remove the tomatoes to a work surface. Use a paring knife to slip the peels off the tomatoes.

This peanut stew combines West African staples (groundnuts, onions, and chilis) to create unrivaled flavor.

I used jalapeño peppers to cut the heat in this recipe. If you want to make traditional jerk chicken, substitute one Scotch bonnet pepper for the jalapeño peppers.

Jamaican Jerk-Spiced Chicken

Jamaican jerk spice refers to a distinctive spice rub used in jerk cooking, a particular cooking technique native to Jamaica (see Jerk Cooking on page 95). The meat is marinated in a spicy paste-like sauce and then slowly cooked over smoky charcoal. This recipe approximates the flavors of the real deal.

Inspiration: Jamaica | **Serves:** 4 to 6 | **Slow cooker time:** 3½ hours

INGREDIENTS

- 1 cup (150g) chopped sweet onions, like Vidalia
- ⅓ cup (34g) chopped scallions
- 1 teaspoon dried thyme or 2 teaspoons fresh thyme
- 1 teaspoon salt
- 1 teaspoon black pepper
- 2 teaspoons sugar
- 1 teaspoon ground allspice
- ½ teaspoon ground nutmeg
- ½ teaspoon ground cinnamon
- 2 whole jalapeño peppers, sliced
- 3 tablespoons (45mL) soy sauce
- 1 tablespoon (15mL) canola oil
- 1 tablespoon (15mL) cider vinegar
- 4 pounds (1.8kg) cut-up chicken pieces, skin removed

1. One day ahead, place all the ingredients except the chicken in the bowl of a food processor. Puree, scraping down the sides of the bowl several times, until the mixture is smooth. Place the chicken in a large freezer-weight zipper bag. Pour the marinade mixture into the bag. Close the bag and massage the chicken so that all the pieces are well coated with marinade. Refrigerate the chicken overnight.

2. To cook, remove the chicken from the marinade and place it in a 4-quart (3.8L) slow cooker. Discard the marinade. Cook on the low setting for 3½ hours, until the chicken has cooked through but is not falling off the bone.

3. Preheat a gas grill to medium-hot, about 450°F (230°C). Sear the chicken for 2½ minutes per side. Serve immediately.

Jerk Cooking

Jerk cooking originated in Jamaica long ago, a fusion of African and Taino cultures. The Tainos were part of Jamaica's indigenous population. They called the island "Xaymaca," which meant "land of wood and water." Their first contact with Europeans came in 1494, when Columbus arrived. Fifteen years later, the Spanish colonized the island, bringing with them enslaved black labor. In the middle of the seventeenth century, the British arrived and the Spanish fled to a settlement in Cuba. Those who had been enslaved by the Spanish fled to the mountains and became known as the Maroons. ("Maroon" was a derivative of the Spanish word *cimarrones*, meaning mountaineers.) They settled among the Tainos in the mountainous regions of the island, where they shared culinary traditions. One of those traditions was the art of jerking.

The word "jerk" is said to come from the Spanish word *charqui*, or dried meat. The Tainos taught the Maroons to preserve meats by puncturing the meat and stuffing the holes with a variety of spices. Then the meat was cooked in a deep pit lined with stones over burning pimento (allspice) wood, which gave it a unique smoky flavor. According to Jamaica's official culinary authorities, for a dish to be classified as "authentic jerk," the meat "must be smoked over pimento wood." In present-day jerking, the chosen meat is marinated in a spicy paste-like sauce that includes allspice and Scotch bonnet peppers, and then is smoked in a steel-drum jerk pan or in a wood-burning oven.

The most common jerk cooking equipment these days is usually made from a modified oil barrel with a hinged lid.

Sun-Dried Tomato and Mushroom Sauced Chicken

Before modern food preservation methods, Italians dried the summer's bounty of tomatoes in the sun on their ceramic rooftop tiles for use during the winter months. It took four to ten days for the sun-drying process to take place. It takes 20 pounds (9kg) of tomatoes to produce 1 pound (454g) of sun-dried tomatoes. Serve this saucy chicken over orzo, penne, or mini ravioli.

Inspiration: Italy | **Serves:** 6 | **Slow cooker time:** 4 hours

INGREDIENTS

- 2½ pounds (1.2kg) skinless, boneless chicken breasts, cut into ½-inch (1.5cm) slices
- 1 teaspoon salt
- ½ teaspoon black pepper
- 3 tablespoons (43g) butter
- 2 pounds (1kg) white button mushroom caps, wiped clean and thinly sliced
- ⅔ cup (100g) minced shallots
- ½ cup (27g) slivered sun-dried tomatoes
- 2 tablespoons (16g) flour
- ¾ cup (180mL) chicken broth
- ¼ cup (60mL) dry white wine
- 3 tablespoons (12g) snipped fresh parsley

1. Place the chicken breast slices in a 4-quart (3.8L) slow cooker. Sprinkle them with salt and pepper and toss to combine.

2. Melt the butter in a large nonstick skillet over medium heat. Add the mushrooms, shallots, and sun-dried tomatoes. Sauté the mixture, stirring frequently, for 5 minutes, until the mushrooms are soft and have released their liquid. Stir in the flour. Slowly stir in the broth and wine. Transfer the mushroom mixture to the slow cooker. Toss it with the chicken until well combined.

3. Cover the slow cooker and cook on the low setting for 3 hours. Stir the mixture, re-cover it, and cook for 1 hour more. Sprinkle each serving with ½ tablespoon (2g) fresh parsley.

Do not use oil-packed sun-dried tomatoes in this recipe. Instead, use the plain sun-dried tomatoes you'll find packaged in the produce section of your supermarket.

These sauce ingredients combine to create a caramelized depth of flavor.

The sweetness of the apricots and oranges enhances the pungency of the fennel and olives to transform this chicken dish from ho-hum to otherworldly.

Lebanese Orange-Apricot Chicken

The Mediterranean Rim is Europe's best source of fresh and dried fruits as well as the world's olive provider. This dish defies national borders. You could find a similar dish in Israel, Turkey, and other countries of the Mediterranean Rim region. Serve the dish with the Lebanese anise-flavored liquor, arak. Usually served in a small glass, arak, which is a clear liquid, is mixed with several spoonfuls of water, which turns it milky. Watch out, though. The drinks go down smoothly but deliver quite a wallop!

Inspiration: Lebanon | **Serves:** 4 to 6 | **Slow cooker time:** 3 hours

INGREDIENTS

- 2 pounds (1kg) skinless, boneless chicken thighs, cut into 1-inch (2.5-cm) chunks
- 5 large cloves peeled garlic, crushed
- 1 cup (130g) chopped dried apricots
- ½ cup (90g) chopped pitted Greek black olives

- 1 tablespoon (6g) freshly grated orange peel
- 1 orange, peeled, segmented, and chopped, with juices
- ¼ cup (60mL) apricot preserves
- 3 tablespoons (45mL) orange juice
- 1 tablespoon (15mL) lemon juice

- 2 tablespoons (8g) snipped fresh fennel leaves
- 1 tablespoon (5g) finely minced fennel
- ½ cup (100g) light brown sugar

1. Place the chicken, garlic, apricots, olives, orange peel, orange segments with juice, apricot preserves, orange juice, lemon juice, snipped fennel leaves, and minced fennel in a large bowl. Toss the ingredients until they are well mixed.

2. Transfer the mixture to a 4-quart (3.8L) slow cooker. Sprinkle the brown sugar on top of the chicken mixture. Cover the slow cooker and cook on the low setting for 3 hours, until the chicken is cooked through but not dried out. Serve with orzo, rice, or couscous.

You'll find fresh fennel in the produce section of your supermarket. Fennel is a greenish-white bulb that is sold with its stems and feathery leaves attached. The leaves resemble fresh dill. The fennel bulb has a delicate licorice flavor and is great slivered and added to tossed salad.

Lemon Chardonnay Chicken Florentine

Chicken Florentine made with spinach most likely originated in Renaissance France, where the Medici found it fashionable to hire Tuscan cooks who named their creations after their native country. Chicken Florentine made in Florence, Italy, however, uses artichokes instead of spinach.

Inspiration: France | **Serves:** 6 | **Slow cooker time:** 4½ hours

INGREDIENTS

- 2½ pounds (1.2kg) skinless, boneless chicken breasts, quartered
- 2 teaspoons Fox Point Seasoning (see the tip box below)
- 3 tablespoons (45mL) fresh lemon juice
- 2 tablespoons (15g) capers with juice
- ¾ cup (180mL) chicken broth
- ¼ cup (60mL) chardonnay
- 1 tablespoon (15mL) olive oil
- 2 tablespoons (20g) cornstarch
- Three 1-pound (454g) packages fresh baby spinach, washed and spun dry
- ½ cup (227g) shredded mozzarella

1. Season both sides of the chicken breasts with the Fox Point Seasoning. Place the chicken in a 2-quart (1.9L) slow cooker.

2. Place the lemon juice, capers, chicken broth, and chardonnay in a medium saucepan over medium heat and bring it to a boil.

3. Transfer the sauce to the slow cooker. Stir to combine the sauce with the chicken, then cover and cook on the low setting for 3½ hours. Remove the chicken to a dinner plate.

4. Place the cornstarch in a small bowl. Whisk in ¼ cup (60mL) of the sauce from the slow cooker. Whisk the cornstarch mixture into the sauce in the slow cooker. Return the chicken to the slow cooker. Re-cover the slow cooker and cook for 1 hour more. Reduce the heat to the warm setting.

5. Once ready to serve, place the oil in a large nonstick skillet over medium heat. Add one-third of the spinach to the skillet and sauté until it's barely wilted, about 1 minute, stirring constantly. Use a slotted spoon to remove the spinach and divide it between two dinner plates. Repeat the process twice more with the remaining spinach.

6. Top each of the six portions of spinach with two to three pieces of chicken. Drizzle each portion with the lemon-chardonnay sauce. Sprinkle each serving with shredded mozzarella. Serve immediately.

Fox Point Seasoning is a great combination of salt, dried shallots, dried chives, garlic powder, onion powder, and ground green peppercorns. You can make up your own blend of these spices if you don't want to order the Fox Point Seasoning.

Chicken Florentine is bathed in a rich but refreshing lemon-caper sauce.

This sweet, tangy dish evokes memories of an island-hopping cruise to Barbados, Saint Maarten, and Jamaica.

Island Citrus Chicken

Sweet and tangy, this citrusy sauce dresses up the common backyard chickens often seen roaming the islands of the Caribbean.

Inspiration: Caribbean | **Serves:** 4 | **Slow cooker time:** 3 hours

INGREDIENTS

- 1⅓ to 1½ pounds (605 to 680g) skinless, boneless chicken breasts
- 3 tablespoons (23g) flour
- ½ cup (120mL) orange marmalade
- ½ cup (120mL) shrimp cocktail sauce (bottled)
- 2 teaspoons dry mustard
- ¼ teaspoon curry powder

1. Wash the chicken and pat it dry with paper towels. Place the flour on a dinner plate and dredge both sides of each chicken breast in flour. Transfer the floured chicken breasts to a 2-quart (1.9L) slow cooker.

2. Mix the marmalade, cocktail sauce, dry mustard, and curry powder together in a medium bowl. Pour the sauce over the chicken. Cover the slow cooker and cook on the low setting for 3 hours or until the chicken is cooked through but not dry. (You can hold the chicken on the warm setting for up to 30 minutes.)

3. Slice the chicken breasts lengthwise, then into chunks across the grain. Place the chicken back in the slow cooker and toss it well with the sauce. Transfer the chicken to a serving platter, drizzle any remaining sauce over the top, and serve immediately.

If you don't have bottled cocktail sauce, make your own by adding 1 tablespoon (15mL) of prepared horseradish to ½ cup (120mL) ketchup. Adjust the amount of horseradish to taste.

Chicken Marengo

As the story goes, Napoleon Bonaparte successfully ended his Italian campaign with a victory over Austria in the Battle of Marengo, in Piedmont, Italy, on June 14, 1800. Securing ingredients from local farmers, his personal chef created the original version of this chicken dish for Napoleon's dinner that evening, cooking it while still in the battlefield. Napoleon so loved the dish, he had it prepared after every successful battle.

Inspiration: France | **Serves:** 6 | **Slow cooker time:** 4 hours

INGREDIENTS

- 8 ounces (227g) hot pork sausage
- ½ cup (60g) flour
- Salt and black pepper
- 1 teaspoon dried tarragon
- 3 pounds (1.5kg) skinless, boneless chicken breasts, rinsed and patted dry with paper towels
- 4 tablespoons (56g) butter, divided
- 8 ounces (227g) button mushrooms, wiped clean and sliced
- 1 teaspoon garlic paste or finely minced garlic
- ½ cup (120mL) white wine
- Two 14.5-ounce (411g) cans diced tomatoes with basil, garlic, and oregano, drained, with juices reserved
- ¼ teaspoon onion powder
- 1 pound (454g) pennette (miniature penne pasta)

1. Crumble the sausage in a large nonstick saucepan over medium heat. Cook the sausage, stirring frequently, until it's browned and cooked through. Use a slotted spoon to transfer the sausage to a 5½- to 6-quart (5.2 to 5.7L) slow cooker.

2. Mix the flour, 1 teaspoon (6g) of the salt, ½ teaspoon (1g) of the pepper, and tarragon together on a dinner plate. Dredge the chicken breasts in the flour mixture, coating all the sides. Reserve the excess flour mixture.

3. Melt 2 tablespoons (28g) of the butter in a skillet. Place half the floured chicken breasts in the skillet and sauté them over medium heat until browned, about 1½ minutes per side. Transfer the chicken to the slow cooker. Repeat the process with the remaining chicken breasts.

4. Add the remaining 2 tablespoons (28g) of butter to the skillet. When the butter has melted, add the mushrooms and garlic and sauté for 2 to 3 minutes. Reduce the heat to low. Stir in the remaining flour mixture. Add the wine and ½ cup (120mL) of the reserved juice from the diced tomatoes. Stir until the pan is deglazed and the sauce has thickened, about 30 seconds. Stir in the tomatoes and onion powder. Spoon the mushroom-tomato mixture over the chicken breasts and sausage.

5. Cover the slow cooker and cook on the low setting for 4 hours until the chicken is cooked through but not shredding. Adjust the seasoning with salt and pepper to taste.

6. Bring a large pot of water to boil over high heat. Add the pennette, reduce the heat to medium, and cook according to the manufacturer's instructions until the pasta is al dente, about 8 minutes. Drain the pasta in a colander.

7. Place a portion of the pasta and one chicken breast on each dinner plate. Spoon the sauce over the chicken and pasta. Serve immediately.

If you'd like to add sliced onions to this dish, sauté them with the mushrooms and eliminate the onion powder.

Sweet and spicy, Chicken Marengo is as pleasing to the eye as it is to the palate.

Capers and olives add to the distinctive Mediterranean flair of this dish.

Med-Rim Chicken

The cuisines of the countries rimming the Mediterranean Sea offer a wide variety of different flavor combinations. This dish is reminiscent of meals I enjoyed while traveling in Spain, Portugal, and Greece. Serve the chicken atop a bed of steamed rice or your favorite al dente pasta, then top the whole thing with the piquant sauce.

Inspiration: Mediterranean Rim | **Serves:** 4 to 6 | **Slow cooker time:** 5 hours

INGREDIENTS

- One 4-pound (2kg) chicken, cut into pieces
- 2 to 3 teaspoons Greek seasoning blend (see the tip box below)
- 2 tablespoons (30mL) canola oil
- 2 cups (300g) chopped sweet onions, like Vidalia
- 1 tablespoon (7.5g) capers, rinsed and drained
- ½ cup (60g) pimento-stuffed green olives, cut in half
- ½ cup (75g) golden raisins
- 4 teaspoons garlic paste or finely minced garlic
- 2 tablespoons (30mL) lemon juice
- ½ teaspoon cumin
- 1 teaspoon oregano
- ½ teaspoon (2.5mL) caper juice
- ¼ cup (60mL) dry white wine
- ¼ cup (52g) firmly packed cup brown sugar
- Salt and freshly ground black pepper

1. Wash the chicken, pat it dry with paper towels, and cut off any excess skin and fat. Sprinkle the seasoning blend over both sides of each chicken piece.

2. Place the oil in a large nonstick skillet over medium heat. Place the chicken, skin sides down, in the skillet. Cook for 2 minutes per side, until the chicken is golden brown. Transfer the chicken to a 4- or 5-quart (3.8 or 4.8L) slow cooker.

3. Top the chicken with onions, capers, olives, and raisins. Place the garlic, lemon juice, cumin, oregano, caper juice, and white wine in a small bowl and whisk until smooth. Pour the mixture over the chicken. Sprinkle brown sugar on top of the chicken.

4. Cook on the low setting for 5 hours or until the chicken is tender. Season with salt and pepper to taste before serving.

You can make your own Greek seasoning blend: Mix together 1½ teaspoons of dried oregano, ½ teaspoon of garlic powder, 1 teaspoon of dried lemon peel, ½ teaspoon of dried marjoram, ½ teaspoon of black pepper, ½ teaspoon of salt, and ½ teaspoon of onion powder. Store the mix in an airtight container and use it as needed.

This recipe encompasses all the flavors of a traditional Thanksgiving dinner.

Turkey Breast and Orange-Cranberry Sauce

Succulent turkey enveloped in tart cranberry sauce combines two of the best dishes of a Thanksgiving feast . . . any time of the year.

Inspiration: USA | **Serves:** 4 to 6 | **Slow cooker time:** 6 hours

INGREDIENTS

- One 3-pound (1.5kg) boneless turkey breast roast (I used Butterball)
- 2 cups (240g) fresh cranberries, picked over and rinsed
- 2 tablespoons (24g) sugar
- ⅓ cup (80mL) orange juice concentrate
- 1 tablespoon (6g) grated orange peel
- ½ cup (120mL) chicken broth

This orange-cranberry sauce is thin at first—more like broth. If you'd like a thicker sauce, transfer it to a medium nonstick saucepan over medium heat. Whisk together 1 tablespoon (10g) of cornstarch and 1 tablespoon (15mL) of the orange-cranberry sauce in a small bowl. Whisk this cornstarch mixture into the remaining sauce. Cook the sauce, stirring constantly, until it thickens, 2 to 3 minutes.

1. Place the turkey breast in a 4-quart (3.8L) slow cooker.

2. Place the cranberries in a medium nonstick saucepan over medium heat. Sprinkle them with sugar. Add the orange juice concentrate, orange peel, and chicken broth to the saucepan. Stir to combine the ingredients. Cook, stirring occasionally, until the cranberries pop and the mixture comes to a boil, 4 to 5 minutes.

3. Pour the cranberry mixture over the turkey breast. Cover the slow cooker and cook on the low setting for 6 hours.

4. Transfer the turkey breast to a cutting board and cut it into ½-inch (1.5cm) slices. Transfer the orange-cranberry sauce to a serving bowl. Ladle orange-cranberry sauce atop each serving of turkey.

Cheesy Shredded Potatoes

Reminiscent of the flavor of a French potato gratin, these potatoes
are as comforting as they are easy to prepare.

Inspiration: USA and France | **Serves:** 6 to 8 | **Slow cooker time:** 4 hours

INGREDIENTS

- One 30-ounce (850g) package frozen country-style shredded hash brown potatoes, thawed
- 8 tablespoons (113g) butter, melted (divided)
- One 8-ounce (227g) package shredded sharp cheddar cheese
- One 10¾-ounce (305g) can cream of chicken soup with herbs
- 1½ tablespoons (3g) dried minced onions
- ¾ cup (180mL) sour cream
- 1 cup (15g) fresh breadcrumbs

1. Squeeze the thawed potatoes with paper towels to remove any excess moisture. Place the potatoes in a 4-quart (3.8L) slow cooker. Add ¼ cup (60mL) of the melted butter and the cheese, soup, and dried minced onions. Stir until the ingredients are well combined.

2. Cover the slow cooker and cook on the low temperature for 3½ hours. Stir in the sour cream. Top with the breadcrumbs and drizzle the remaining ¼ cup (60mL) of melted butter over the breadcrumbs.

3. Re-cover the slow cooker and cook the potatoes for 30 minutes more, until the breadcrumbs have browned slightly. You can reduce the heat setting to warm and hold the potatoes for up to 2 hours.

Try working these into your Sunday brunch menu.

Greek Pork Chops

Loaded with classic Greek ingredients, this piquant sauce transforms the everyday American pork chop into company fare. It is important to use very thick, bone-in chops for this recipe. Serve the chops with rice or orzo.

Inspiration: Greece | **Serves:** 2 | **Slow cooker time:** 4 to 4½ hours

INGREDIENTS

- Two 10- to 12-ounce (284 to 340g) bone-in pork chops
- Lemon-herb seasoning
- 1 teaspoon flour
- 1 tablespoon (15mL) plus 1 teaspoon (5mL) olive oil
- 2 cups (200g) halved and thinly sliced sweet onions, like Vidalia
- ½ cup (75g) golden raisins
- 1 tablespoon (14g) garlic paste or finely minced garlic
- ¾ cup (170g) quartered grape tomatoes
- 1 tablespoon (12g) sugar
- 1 teaspoon dried oregano leaves
- ¼ cup (60mL) marsala wine
- ½ cup (120mL) chicken broth
- 2 tablespoons (30mL) white balsamic or white wine vinegar
- ¼ cup (30g) quartered pimento-stuffed green olives
- 1 tablespoon (7.5g) capers, rinsed and drained
- 2 tablespoons (15g) crumbled feta cheese, divided

1. Sprinkle both sides of the pork chops with the lemon-herb seasoning to taste. Place the flour in a small sieve and sprinkle it on both sides of the chops. Place 1 tablespoon (15mL) of the olive oil in a large nonstick skillet over medium heat. Add the chops and sauté for 1½ minutes per side, until browned. Transfer the chops to a 2-quart (1.9L) slow cooker.

2. Add the onions to the skillet over medium heat and sauté them, stirring frequently, for 1½ minutes. Add the raisins and sauté for 30 seconds. Spread the onions and raisins atop the chops.

3. Add 1 teaspoon (5mL) of the olive oil to the skillet over medium heat. Add the garlic and sauté for 30 seconds. Add the tomatoes, sugar, and oregano and sauté for 30 seconds, stirring constantly. Pour in the wine, broth, and vinegar and bring everything to a boil, about 1 minute. Pour the mixture over the chops in the slow cooker. Sprinkle them with the olives and capers.

4. Cover the slow cooker and cook on the low setting for 4 to 4½ hours, until the chops are tender enough to be cut with a sharp knife, but are not shredding. (The chops should be the consistency of a grilled steak.)

5. To serve, place one chop on each dinner plate. Sprinkle each with 1 tablespoon (7.5g) of the feta cheese. Top each with a generous portion of the sauce and serve the remaining sauce on the side.

> *To serve four, double the recipe and use a 4- or 5-quart (3.8 to 4.8L) slow cooker. The cooking time will remain the same as long as the total ingredients fill the slow cooker at least two-thirds full. If the cooker is less than two-thirds full, reduce the cooking time.*

These pork chops are enfolded in classic Greek ingredients—capers, raisins, tomatoes, and onions.

Bold flavors enhance these juicy pork tenderloins.

Cuban-Chinese Barbecued Pork Tenderloin

A common sight hanging in the windows of Chinese restaurants are pork tenderloins that have been roasted with honey, hoisin sauce, Chinese five-spice powder, garlic, sugar, and soy sauce. You wouldn't expect to see this combination in Cuba, where pork is the most plentiful meat, but you would be wrong. In the nineteenth century, hundreds of Chinese laborers worked in Cuba, bringing Asian spices and sauces to the island. In all likelihood, the additional of black beans was a Cuban contribution to this flavorful combination of ingredients.

Inspiration: Cuba and China | **Serves:** 6 to 8 | **Slow cooker time:** 4 hours

INGREDIENTS

- 3 tablespoons (45mL) soy sauce
- 3 tablespoons (45mL) cream sherry
- 2 tablespoons (30mL) hoisin sauce
- ¼ cup (65g) black bean dip
- 2 tablespoons (15g) Chinese five-spice powder
- 2 tablespoons (28g) garlic paste or finely minced garlic
- 3 tablespoons (36g) sugar
- ¼ cup (60mL) honey
- Two 1¼-pound (567g) pork tenderloins

1. Mix the soy sauce, sherry, hoisin sauce, bean dip, five-spice powder, garlic, sugar, and honey in a medium bowl. Rinse the tenderloins and pat them dry with paper towels. Spoon enough sauce over both sides of each tenderloin to cover them.

2. Place the tenderloins in a 1½- or 2-quart (1.4 or 1.9L) slow cooker. Pour the remaining sauce over the pork. Cover the slow cooker and cook on the low setting for 4 hours, until the pork has cooked through but is not shredding.

3. Remove the tenderloins and cut them into ½-inch (1.5cm) slices. Drizzle the sauce over the pork and serve immediately.

Garlic and honey enhance the other powerhouse ingredients to add a savory sweetness to the sauce.

Indochine Pineapple Pork

At the same time sweet and spicy, this recipe showcases the flavors of Indochina—pineapple, hot chilis, tomato, tamarind, coconut, and peanuts. Indochina is a region of Southeast Asia, east of India and southwest of China, that comprises Cambodia, Laos, Myanmar, Thailand, and Vietnam. The name "Indochine" was coined by French colonizers as a contraction of India and China.

Inspiration: Indochina | **Serves:** 4 to 6 | **Slow cooker time:** 5 hours

INGREDIENTS

- 1 cup (240mL) sweetened cream of coconut (I used Coco López)
- ½ cup (120mL) pineapple juice
- ¼ cup (60mL) tamarind syrup
- ¼ cup (60mL) Asian sweet chili sauce
- 1 tablespoon (14g) Thai chili garlic paste
- ¼ cup (6omL) teriyaki sauce
- 2 tablespoons (30mL) soy sauce
- 2 tablespoons (30mL) rice wine vinegar
- 3 tablespoons (45mL) honey
- 2 tablespoons (30mL) peanut butter
- ½ cup (60g) flour
- 2 pounds (1kg) pork loin roast, cut into 1-inch (2.5cm) pieces
- Salt and freshly ground black pepper
- 1 tablespoon (15mL) olive oil
- 2 cups (300g) chopped onions
- 2 tablespoons (28g) garlic paste or finely minced garlic
- 2 cups (450g) fresh pineapple, cut into 1-inch (2.5cm) pieces
- One 14.5-ounce (411g) can petite-diced tomatoes, drained

1. Up to 2 weeks ahead, prepare the Indochine sauce. Place the cream of coconut, pineapple juice, tamarind syrup, and sweet chili sauce in a blender and pulse until smooth. Add the chili garlic paste, teriyaki and soy sauces, vinegar, and honey and pulse until smooth. Add the peanut butter and pulse until smooth. Transfer the sauce to a covered container until needed. (Makes 3 cups [710mL].)

2. Place the flour in a freezer-weight zipper bag. Add the pork pieces in batches, closing the bag and shaking each batch until the pork is well coated with flour. Shake off any excess flour and transfer the floured pork to a dinner plate. Season it with salt and pepper to taste.

3. Place the oil in a large nonstick skillet over medium heat. Add the pork in batches and cook until it's browned, 2 to 3 minutes. Transfer the pork to a 4-quart (3.8L) slow cooker.

4. Add the onions and garlic to the skillet and sauté them until the onions have softened and browned slightly, about 2 minutes. Transfer them to the slow cooker.

5. Add the pineapple, tomatoes, and 1 cup (240mL) of the Indochine sauce to the slow cooker. Stir to combine the ingredients. Cover the slow cooker and cook on the low setting for 5 hours, until the pork has cooked through and is tender when tested with the point of a knife.

6. Serve the pork and sauce with Persian Rice (see the recipe on page 158).

The Indochine sauce also makes a wonderful marinade for beef, chicken, or shrimp. Used sparingly, the sauce is also great drizzled atop a vegetable salad.

Tamarind syrup is made from the fruit of the tamarind tree. You can order it through online retailers. One bottle will last you a lifetime.

This simple five ingredient sauce adds a sweet, yet, tangy note to the braised pork.

Autumn Harvest Pork Roast

Sauced with the fruits of a fall harvest—apples and cranberries—this pork dish is packed with flavor and as colorful as an autumn day.

Inspiration: North America | **Serves:** 4 to 6 | **Slow cooker time:** 4 hours

INGREDIENTS

- ½ tablespoon (7.5mL) olive oil
- 2- to 2½-pound (1 to 1.2kg) boneless pork loin rib end roast
- One 12-ounce (340g) package frozen Stouffer's Harvest Apples, thawed
- One 14-ounce (397g) can whole-berry cranberry sauce
- 1 cup (240mL) Catalina salad dressing
- 2 tablespoons (14g) dry onion soup mix

1. Place the oil in a large nonstick skillet over medium heat. When the oil is hot, add the pork loin and brown it on all sides, about 3 minutes. Transfer the pork to a 4-quart (3.8L) slow cooker.

2. Microwave the apples according to the manufacturer's instructions, about 5 minutes. Mix the cranberry sauce, salad dressing, onion soup mix, and apples together in a medium bowl. Pour the mixture over the pork loin. Cover the slow cooker and cook on the low setting for 4 hours.

3. To serve, thinly slice the pork and serve it topped with the fruit sauce. Serve the remaining sauce on the side.

Apples and cranberries add the flavors of the autumn season.

Pork Chops and Onions in *Gado-Gado* Sauce

Gado-gado is a traditional Indonesian dish consisting of a vegetable salad topped with peanut sauce dressing. In this recipe, thick pork chops and sliced onions slowly simmer in a sweet, citrusy gado-gado–style peanut sauce. If you'd like a little fire in your sauce, add a couple of teaspoons of Asian sweet chili sauce.

Inspiration: Indonesia | **Serves:** 4 | **Slow cooker time:** 6 to 7 hours

INGREDIENTS

- ⅓ cup (80mL) peanut butter
- ⅓ cup (80mL) frozen orange juice concentrate, defrosted
- ⅓ cup (80mL) honey
- 2 teaspoons garlic paste or finely minced garlic
- 2 teaspoons gingerroot paste or finely minced gingerroot
- 1 tablespoon (15mL) soy sauce
- 2 teaspoons seasoned salt (see the tip box below)
- Four 1½-inch (4cm) thick bone-in pork chops
- 1 tablespoon (15mL) olive oil
- 3 cups (300g) sliced sweet onions, like Vidalia

1. Mix the peanut butter, orange juice concentrate, honey, garlic, gingerroot, and soy sauce together in a medium bowl. Set it aside.

2. Sprinkle the seasoned salt over both sides of each pork chop. Rub the seasoned salt into the chops. Place the oil in a large nonstick skillet over medium heat. When the oil is hot, add the pork chops and sear each side, about 30 seconds per side. Remove the chops from the skillet and place them on a dinner plate.

3. Place half of the sliced onions in the bottom of a 4-quart (3.8L) slow cooker. Dip two of the pork chops into the peanut sauce, liberally coating both sides. Place the chops atop the onions in the slow cooker. Add the remaining onions to the slow cooker in an even layer. Dip the remaining two pork chops into the peanut sauce, liberally coating both sides. Place the chops atop the onions. Pour the remaining sauce over the pork chops and onions.

4. Cover the slow cooker and cook on the low setting for 6 to 7 hours, until the chops are tender but not falling apart. Serve the chops topped with the onions and drizzled with the peanut sauce. Serve the remaining sauce on the side.

I like to use a seasoned salt that is a mixture of sea salt, sugar, black pepper, paprika, onion, turmeric, and garlic. You can substitute your own favorite seasoning blend.

Gado-gado sauce is a sweet citrusy Indonesian peanut sauce.

The combo of pork and sauerkraut is as German as you can get!

Sauerkraut and Pork Chops

Sauerkraut is finely cut raw cabbage that has been layered with salt and left to ferment, a process called lactic acid fermentation. My German grandmother's secret to cooking with sauerkraut was to thoroughly wash and drain it before cooking it with a bit of sugar.

Inspiration: Germany | **Serves:** 6 | **Slow cooker time:** 4½ to 5 hours

INGREDIENTS

- 1 tablespoon (15mL) olive oil
- Six 1-inch (2.5cm) thick boneless pork chops
- Salt and black pepper
- 1 cup (150g) chopped sweet onions, like Vidalia
- One 32-ounce (907g) bag sauerkraut, rinsed and drained
- 2 cups (235g) diced peeled apples
- ½ cup (100g) brown sugar
- ⅛ teaspoon ground cloves
- ¾ cup (180mL) cranberry or cherry honey mustard

1. Place the olive oil in a large nonstick skillet over medium heat. Season the pork chops with salt and black pepper to taste. Sear both sides of the pork chops in the hot skillet until browned, about 3 minutes. Remove the pork chops from the skillet and set them aside.

2. Place the onions in the skillet and sauté them until softened, about 2 minutes. Transfer the onions to a large bowl. Add the sauerkraut, apples, brown sugar, ¼ teaspoon (0.5g) of black pepper, and cloves to the bowl. Toss to mix the ingredients.

3. Place one-third of the sauerkraut mixture in the bottom of a 5-quart (4.8L) slow cooker. Place the seared pork chops atop the sauerkraut mixture. Spread the remaining two-thirds of the sauerkraut mixture on top of the chops.

4. Cover the slow cooker and cook on the low setting for 4½ to 5 hours until the pork chops are tender enough to be cut with a sharp knife. Remove the chops from the slow cooker. Season the sauerkraut mixture with salt and pepper to taste. Serve the pork chops on a bed of sauerkraut.

Sweet onions lack the sharp flavor of other onions. Their mildness is attributable to a low sulfur content and a high water content. Only buy as many sweet onions as you can use in a two-week period and refrigerate them.

Russian Cherry Orchard Pork Stew

As witnessed in Chekhov's *The Cherry Orchard*, Russians love cherries, which grow profusely in the country's central region. This pork simmers to fork-tenderness, absorbing the subtle sweetness of the cherries.

Inspiration: Russia | **Serves:** 4 to 6 | **Slow cooker time:** 4½ hours

INGREDIENTS

- ¼ cup (30g) flour
- 1 tablespoon (12g) lemon-herb seasoning
- 2½ pounds (1.2kg) pork loin roast, cut into 1-inch (2.5cm) cubes
- 4 tablespoons (57g) butter, divided
- 1½ cups (225g) chopped sweet onions, like Vidalia
- Two 20-ounce (567g) cans no-sugar-added cherry pie filling, divided
- 1 teaspoon salt
- 3 tablespoons (45mL) lemon juice
- ⅛ teaspoon ground nutmeg
- ½ teaspoon crushed red pepper flakes
- One 16-ounce (454g) can large butter beans, rinsed and drained
- 1½ to 2 teaspoons (7.5 to 10mL) browning sauce (I used Kitchen Bouquet® Browning & Seasoning Sauce)
- Snipped fresh herbs, optional

1. Place the flour and lemon-herb seasoning in a freezer-weight zipper bag. Add the pork pieces in batches, closing the bag and shaking until the pork is well coated with flour. Shake off any excess flour and transfer the floured pork to a dinner plate.

2. Place 2 tablespoons (28.5g) of the butter in a large nonstick skillet over medium heat. Add half the pork and cook it until browned, 2 to 3 minutes. Transfer the pork to a 4-quart (3.8L) slow cooker. Add the remaining 2 tablespoons (28.5g) of butter to the skillet and brown the remaining pork. Transfer the pork to the slow cooker. Sprinkle any remaining flour and seasoning over the pork.

3. Add the onions to the skillet and sauté them until the onions have softened and browned slightly, about 3 minutes. Transfer them to the slow cooker. Add one can of pie filling, salt, lemon juice, nutmeg, and red pepper flakes to the slow cooker. Stir to combine the ingredients. Top everything with the remaining can of pie filling.

4. Cover the slow cooker and cook on the low heat setting for 4 hours. Add the butter beans and stir to combine. Re-cover the slow cooker and cook for 30 minutes. Stir in the browning sauce until the stew is a ruby-tinged bronze color. Serve immediately. Garnish with fresh herbs, if desired.

The pie filling's cherry sweetness enchances the flavor of the pork loin in this stew.

The stew tastes even better if it is made a day ahead and the flavors are allowed to marry overnight.

These Mexican-style tacos are smokin' hot!

Slow-Roasted Chipotle Pork Tacos

Spicyyyyyyyy! This savory pork gets tamed when smothered with guacamole and sour cream in corn tortillas. These Mexican tacos are smokin' hot! You may want to add a bucket of Mexican *cervezas*, like Corona® or Dos Equis®, to the sideboard so your guests can put out the chipotle fire.

Inspiration: Mexico | **Serves:** 4 (three tacos each) or 6 (two tacos each) | **Slow cooker time:** 6 to 6½ hours

INGREDIENTS

- 3 tablespoons (41g) coarse salt
- 1 tablespoon (6g) chipotle chili powder
- 3- to 3½-pound (1.4 to 1.6kg) pork loin roast
- 24 small corn or flour tortillas
- 2 cups (480mL) guacamole
- 2 cups (480mL) sour cream
- 2 cups (480mL) fresh mild salsa
- 2 limes, cut into wedges
- ½ cup (25g) snipped fresh cilantro

1. Mix the salt and chipotle chili powder together in a small bowl. Sprinkle the mixture on all sides of the pork roast, rubbing it into the surface of the meat.

2. Place the pork in a 5-quart (4.8L) slow cooker. Cook on the low setting for 6- to 6½ hours, until the pork shreds when tested with a fork. Transfer the pork to a large platter and use two forks to shred it. Cover the shredded pork with aluminum foil.

3. Heat the tortillas on a medium-hot griddle or in a large nonstick skillet over medium heat, turning them frequently with tongs until they are heated through and soft. Stack the tortillas and wrap them in a large cloth napkin. Place the wrapped tortillas in a basket.

4. To serve, remove the foil from the platter of pork. Serve along with the basket of tortillas, the lime wedges, and bowls of guacamole, sour cream, salsa, and cilantro. Allow diners to assemble their own tacos.

You can build your tacos as you prefer, but I suggest starting your tacos by placing two tortillas (one on top of the other) on a dinner plate. Spread the top tortilla with guacamole and sour cream, then place a portion of chipotle pork on top. Squeeze lime juice over the pork and sprinkle everything with the salsa and cilantro. Fold the double tortilla in half and enjoy!

You can hold the pork, once shredded, for up to 2 hours. Return the pulled pork to the sauce in the slow cooker and reduce the heat setting to warm. The pork will take on the flavor of the cooking sauce more intensely, so you may want to serve the Battle Sauces on the side or eliminate them.

Pulled Pork Tenderloin

North Carolinians are justly proud of their pulled pork, usually made using a whole pig slow cooked outside over hot coals. This recipe, slow cooked inside in any weather, uses pork tenderloin, which provides the best meat yield with minimum fat content. The sauce war carries on, however, no matter how the pork is slow cooked. The eastern part of the state prefers a spicy vinegar sauce, while the western mountain region insists on a sweeter red sauce. Make both sauces on page 127, and you be the judge.

Inspiration: USA | **Serves:** 10 to 12 | **Slow cooker time:** 4½ to 5 hours

INGREDIENTS

- 1 tablespoon (15mL) olive oil
- Salt and black pepper
- One 5-pound (2.5kg) package pork tenderloins
- 3 large sweet onions, like Vidalia, cut in half and thinly sliced
- ⅔ cup (160mL) ketchup

- ⅔ cup (160mL) chicken broth
- 4 teaspoons (18g) garlic paste or finely minced garlic
- ¼ cup (60mL) apple cider vinegar
- 2 tablespoons (30mL) Worcestershire sauce
- 1 teaspoon chili powder

- ½ teaspoon dry mustard
- ½ teaspoon (2.5mL) Tabasco® sauce
- Prepared coleslaw, optional for serving

1. Place the olive oil in a large nonstick skillet over medium heat. Season the tenderloins with salt and pepper. Place the tenderloins in the skillet and sear it on all sides, about 2 minutes in total. Transfer the tenderloins to a 5- or 6-quart (4.8 or 5.7L) slow cooker. Top them with onions.

2. Whisk the ketchup, broth, garlic, vinegar, Worcestershire sauce, chili powder, dry mustard, and Tabasco sauce together in a medium bowl. Pour the mixture over the tenderloins. Cover the slow cooker and cook on the low setting for 4 to 5 hours, until the tenderloins can be shredded with a fork.

3. Remove the tenderloins from the sauce. Use a fork to shred the pork. Use a slotted spoon to remove the onions from the slow cooker. Chop the onions and toss them with the pork.

4. Serve the pork, sprinkled with your choice of Battle Sauce (see the recipes below), on toasted Kaiser or hamburger rolls. Top with coleslaw if desired.

North Carolina Battle Sauces

The Hatfields and the McCoys had nothin' on the folks of North Carolina when it came to feuding. The battle over the "proper" barbecue sauce for pulled pork in this southern state goes on to this day.

No matter which sauce you make, it will pack a flavorful punch.

Inspiration: USA | **Makes:** 1 cup (240mL)

Eastern North Carolina Barbecue Sauce

INGREDIENTS
- 1 cup (240mL) apple cider vinegar
- 1 teaspoon (6g) salt
- 1 teaspoon (2g) cayenne pepper
- 1 tablespoon (6g) crushed red pepper flakes
- 1 tablespoon (6g) freshly ground black pepper

1. Two days ahead, place all the ingredients in a glass jar. Secure the lid and shake well. Refrigerate the sauce for two days to allow the flavors to marry. (The sauce will keep, refrigerated, for up to one month.)

2. Serve at room temperature.

Western North Carolina Barbecue Sauce

INGREDIENTS
- 2 tablespoons (28.5g) butter
- ½ cup (104g) packed brown sugar
- ½ cup (120mL) ketchup
- ¼ cup (60mL) fresh lemon juice
- ½ teaspoon (2.5mL) hot pepper sauce
- ½ teaspoon (2.5mL) Worcestershire sauce
- 3 tablespoons (10g) finely minced sweet onions, like Vidalia

1. Melt the butter in a small saucepan over medium-low heat. Whisk in the brown sugar until it dissolves. Whisk in the ketchup, lemon juice, hot pepper and Worcestershire sauces, and onions. Reduce the heat to low and cook, stirring occasionally, until the sauce thickens, about 10 minutes.

2. Serve immediately or transfer to a covered container and refrigerate until needed. (The sauce will keep, refrigerated, for up to two weeks.)

To gently reheat the sauce before serving, place it in a microwave-safe container and microwave for 30 seconds.

Brats 'n' Beer

Simmering the bratwurst slowly in beer and onions cooks the sausages from the inside out, which keeps them juicy when finished on a hot grill. Placing them back in the simmering brew guarantees the brats stay moist until they are devoured.

Inspiration: Germany | **Serves:** 6 to 8 | **Slow cooker time:** 2 hours

INGREDIENTS

- 12 bratwurst
- Three 12-ounce (340g) cans beer
- 4 cups (400g) sliced onions

1. Place the bratwurst, beer, and onions in a 5- or 6-quart (4.8 or 5.7L) slow cooker. Cook on the low setting for 2 hours. Remove the bratwurst from the slow cooker with tongs. (Do not puncture the skin or the filling will ooze out.) Reduce the heat setting to warm.

2. Preheat a gas grill. Cook the bratwurst on the hot grill for 3 minutes on each side, turning carefully with tongs, until browned. Place the grilled bratwurst back in the slow cooker, submerged in the beer and onions, until serving, for up to 4 hours.

3. Serve the bratwurst on toasted buns, with ketchup, mustard, sauerkraut, and chopped onions.

German Bratwurst

All bratwurst are sausages, but not all sausages are bratwurst! Bratwurst (pronounced *braaht wurst*) are German sausages usually made from ground pork and spices (although sometimes beef or veal is also added). The first documented evidence of bratwurst in Germany dates back to the early 1300s. Farmers would encase scraps of meat in a thin casing made of animal intestines. They would make the sausages in the morning and eat them by noon because they spoiled so quickly.

Bratwurst is a German word coming from *braten* (to pan fry or roast) and *wurst* (sausage). The sausages vary by region in Germany, and each recipe is culturally different. How they are served is different as well, although most commonly they are served in a wheat roll with mustard or sauerkraut. Bratwurst came to North America with German immigrants, who mainly settled in the Upper Midwest. Wisconsin, where a great number of Germans settled in the early nineteenth century, is known for its bratwurst. Since 1953, Sheboygan has held an annual Brat Days Festival, where there is a brat-eating contest, beer, live music, a parade, rides, and every kind of bratwurst imaginable. The recipe above is the Sheboygan style.

I like Johnsonville Original Brats, which most closely look and taste like those you'd get from a 'wurst-country butcher.

This classic combination is perfect for summer celebrations.

Hoisin-Ginger Barbecued Baby Back Ribs

A nice change from the tomato-based barbecue sauces usually served with ribs, this Asian-inspired sauce is light, sweet, and spicy. The method of first slow cooking the ribs before grilling them guarantees moist, juicy ribs every time.

Inspiration: China | **Serves:** 6 to 8 | **Slow cooker time:** 5 hours

INGREDIENTS

- Spice rub of choice
- 5 pounds (2.5kg) baby back ribs (2 racks, each cut into thirds)
- ½ cup (120mL) hoisin sauce
- 3 tablespoons (45mL) rice vinegar
- 3 tablespoons (45mL) soy sauce
- 1 tablespoon (15mL) sesame oil
- 1 tablespoon (11g) finely minced crystallized ginger
- 2 teaspoons garlic paste or finely minced garlic
- 1 teaspoon Chinese five-spice powder

This sauce is light and flavorful, perfect for a family picnic.

1. Liberally sprinkle the spice rub over the top of the ribs. Rub it into the meat with clean hands. Place the ribs in a 5- or 6-quart (4.8 or 5.7L) slow cooker and cook on the low setting for 5 hours, until a knife inserted through the meat cuts easily but the meat is not falling off the bone. (You can hold the ribs for up to 2 hours on the warm setting.)

2. When the ribs are almost done, place the hoisin sauce, vinegar, soy sauce, sesame oil, ginger, garlic, and five-spice powder in a small nonstick saucepan over low heat. Cook the mixture for 8 minutes, stirring frequently, until the sauce is thick and smooth. Remove the sauce from the heat and transfer it to a small bowl.

3. Preheat a gas grill to 450 to 500°F (230 to 260°C). Place the rib racks on the grill, using the indirect cooking method (see the tip in the box below). Spread the sauce on top of the ribs. Grill them for 10 minutes. Turn the ribs over and grill for 2 minutes more. Turn ribs right side up, spread them with more sauce, and grill for 8 minutes more.

4. Cut the racks into individual ribs and serve immediately with any remaining hoisin-ginger sauce on the side.

To use the indirect grilling method, do not turn on the burners under the meat being cooked. Instead, turn on the burners on either side of the meat and place an aluminum foil drip pan underneath the meat to collect any fat and juices so that they do not burn.

Hawaiian Candied Tomatoes

Tomato lovers rejoice! These decadently sweet tomatoes—a favorite in the islands of our fiftieth state—taste almost like dessert. They are the perfect complement for the gingery ribs.

Inspiration: USA | **Serves:** 4 | **Slow cooker time:** 2 to 2½ hours

INGREDIENTS

- 4 small ripe tomatoes
- Salt
- 2 tablespoons (28g) butter
- ½ cup (75g) chopped sweet onions, like Vidalia
- ¼ cup (50g) light brown sugar
- 2 teaspoons (10mL) honey
- ¼ teaspoon black pepper
- 1 cup (15g) fresh breadcrumbs
- 2 teaspoons Parmesan cheese

1. Cut the top quarter off the stem end of each tomato. Scoop out the seeds and liquid from the seed cavities with a small spoon, taking care not to break the flesh between each cavity. Sprinkle the inside of each tomato with salt and turn them upside down on paper towels to drain.

2. Melt the butter in a small nonstick skillet over medium heat. Add the onions and sauté them until softened, about 2 minutes. Stir in the brown sugar, honey, ¼ teaspoon of the salt, and pepper. Add the breadcrumbs and stir until they are well coated with the butter sauce.

3. Using a small spoon, stuff each tomato with one-quarter of the breadcrumb mixture, tucking it into the seed cavities and mounding the stuffing in the tomato.

4. Coat a 1½-quart (1.4L) slow cooker with vegetable cooking spray. Place the tomatoes in the slow cooker, cover it, and cook on the low setting for 2 to 2½ hours, until the tomatoes have softened but are not mushy.

5. Hold on the warm setting for up to 30 minutes or serve immediately. Sprinkle the top of each stuffed tomato with ½ teaspoon of the Parmesan cheese.

Make fresh breadcrumbs in your food processor using leftover bits of bread. Store the crumbs in a zipper bag in the freezer until needed.

To serve 6 to 8, double the recipe and place the tomatoes in a slow cooker that can accommodate them in a single layer. The cooking time remains the same.

These flavorful tomatoes taste almost like candy.

Memphis Barbecued Country-Style Ribs

An old friend of mine, who attended Memphis State, gave this recipe to me decades ago, swearing that it is the best barbecue recipe in Memphis. The lip-smackingly good sauce is great with pulled pork, too (see the recipe on page 126), but don't let a North Carolinian catch you saucing it that way!

Inspiration: USA | **Serves:** 4 | **Slow cooker time:** 5 hours (ribs), 4 hours (sauce)

INGREDIENTS

- 4 to 5 pounds (1.8 to 2.5kg) country-style pork ribs
- Seasoning spice blend
- 1 tablespoon (14g) butter
- ¾ cup (115g) chopped sweet onions, like Vidalia
- One 28-ounce (794g) bottle Open Pit® Original Barbecue Sauce
- 4 teaspoons (20mL) Worcestershire sauce
- 2 teaspoons (3g) dry mustard
- 2 tablespoons (26g) brown sugar
- ⅓ cup (80mL) ketchup
- 4 teaspoon (20mL) white wine vinegar
- Garlic powder
- Lemon-pepper seasoning

1. Sprinkle the seasoning spice blend liberally on all sides of each rib. Place the ribs in a 5-quart (4.8L) slow cooker. Cover the slow cooker and cook on the low setting for 5 hours, or until the ribs are tender when poked with a fork but not falling off the bone. (You can hold the ribs in the slow cooker for up to 2 hours on the warm setting.)

2. Melt the butter in a medium nonstick skillet over medium heat. Add the onions and sauté them, stirring frequently, until they're soft, about 3 minutes. Transfer the onions to a medium bowl.

3. Add the barbecue sauce, Worcestershire sauce, dry mustard, brown sugar, ketchup, and vinegar to the skillet and stir to combine the ingredients. Add the garlic powder and lemon-pepper seasoning to taste.

4. Transfer the sauce mixture to a 1½-quart (1.4L) slow cooker. Cover the slow cooker and cook on the low setting for 4 hours, until the sauce is thick and the flavors have married. (You can hold the sauce in the slow cooker on the warm setting for 2 to 2½ hours.)

5. To serve, preheat a gas grill to medium hot, about 450°F (230°C). Remove the ribs from the slow cooker and place them on a platter. Brush each with barbecue sauce. Place the ribs on the grill with the sauced side down and cook them for 6 minutes. Baste the ribs and turn them over. Baste the tops of the ribs and cook them for 6 minutes more. Serve the ribs with hot barbecue sauce on the side.

Open Pit Barbecue Sauce is essential in this recipe. If your local supermarkets do not carry it, you can order it online.

Memphis-style ribs are lip-smackin', finger-lickin' good!

These Sloppy Joes are bathed in a sauce that is sweet and spicy at the same time.

Sloppy Joes

How this sandwich filling got its name is still a mystery, although many credit it as an invention of Sloppy Joe's Bar in Havana, Cuba. If true, the original was probably picadillo, a distant cousin of the Americanized version (see the recipe on page 65). The ideal stateside Sloppy Joe is sweet and spicy at the same time, with a thick, rich sauce—just like this recipe!

Inspiration: USA | **Serves:** 8 to 10 | **Slow cooker time:** 4 hours

INGREDIENTS

- 1 pound (454g) spicy pork sausage
- 1½ pounds (680g) lean ground beef
- 1 cup (150g) chopped sweet onions
- ½ cup (90g) chopped red bell pepper
- One 6-ounce (170g) can basil, garlic, and oregano tomato paste
- ½ cup (120mL) ketchup
- ¼ cup (52g) packed brown sugar
- 2 tablespoons (30mL) cider vinegar
- 2 tablespoons (30mL) Dijon mustard
- 1 tablespoon (6g) chili powder
- 1 tablespoon (15mL) Worcestershire sauce
- ½ teaspoon salt

1. Crumble the sausage in a large nonstick skillet over medium heat. Sauté, stirring frequently, until browned, about 5 minutes. Drain in a colander. Add the ground beef, onions, and bell pepper to the skillet. Sauté the mixture, stirring frequently, for 5 minutes or until the beef is browned. Drain the mixture in a colander.

2. Transfer the sausage and beef mixture from the colander to a 4-quart (3.8L) slow cooker. Add the tomato paste, ketchup, brown sugar, vinegar, mustard, chili powder, Worcestershire sauce, and salt. Stir to combine the ingredients.

3. Cover the slow cooker and cook on the low setting for 4 hours. Stir the mixture, re-cover it, and turn the heat setting to warm for up to 2 hours, until serving.

4. Serve on hamburger or slider-style buns.

Red bell peppers are the most nutrient-packed of the bell peppers.

PASTA, SAUCES, AND SIDES

Just like meat-focused main dishes, cooking pasta, sauces, and sides in your slow cooker allows you to conveniently infuse the ingredients with layers of flavor over time.

VEGETARIAN ITEMS

Positano, on the Amalfi Coast of Italy, is a popular tourist attraction because of its picturesque appeal and its Mediterranean climate and cuisine.

Literally translated, manicotti means "little muffs."

Chicken and Sausage Manicotti

These baked, stuffed pasta tubes couldn't be easier to prepare. You can make up the filling in advance and freeze it until needed. And best of all, you don't have to boil the dried pasta before assembling the manicotti. Simply stuff the dried tubes, place them in the slow cooker covered with sauce, and walk away!

Inspiration: Italy | **Serves:** 6 to 8 | **Slow cooker time:** 4 to 5 hours

INGREDIENTS

- 4 ounces (113g) skinless, boneless chicken breast, cut into ½-inch (1.5cm) pieces
- 4 ounces (113g) spicy pork sausage, crumbled
- 2 cups (150g) thinly sliced shiitake or button mushrooms
- ¾ cup (130g) diced red bell peppers
- ½ teaspoon cracked black pepper
- ¼ teaspoon coarse salt
- 1 tablespoon (14g) garlic paste or finely minced garlic
- 1 teaspoon Italian seasoning or dry Italian salad dressing mix
- 1 cup (100g) grated Gruyère cheese
- ¾ cup (180g) ricotta cheese
- ¾ cup (68g) grated Parmesan cheese
- ½ cup (52g) sliced scallions
- One 8-ounce (227g) package dried manicotti shells
- 32 ounces (950mL) marinara sauce
- One 8-ounce (227g) package shredded mozzarella cheese

1. Place the chicken and pork sausage in a large skillet over medium heat. Sauté for 2 minutes, until the meat is browned. Add the mushrooms, diced peppers, black pepper, salt, garlic, and Italian seasoning. Cook for 5 minutes, stirring frequently, until the vegetables are soft and the moisture released from the mushrooms has evaporated. Transfer the mixture to a large bowl and allow it to cool for 5 minutes.

2. Mix the cheeses and scallions together in a medium bowl. Fold the cheese mixture into the chicken mixture.

3. Place 1 cup (240mL) of the marinara sauce in the bottom of a 4-quart (3.8L) slow cooker. Using a small spoon, stuff each dried manicotti tube with the chicken and cheese mixture. Place half the stuffed manicotti tubes in a single layer in the slow cooker. Spread 1 cup (240mL) of the marinara sauce on top of the stuffed manicotti. Add a second layer of stuffed pasta. Spread the remaining 2 cups (480mL) of sauce on top.

4. Cover the slow cooker and cook on the low setting for 4 to 5 hours, until the manicotti are soft and the sauce has thickened. Reduce the heat setting to warm. Sprinkle mozzarella atop the manicotti, replace the cover, and allow the cheese to melt (about 15 minutes) before serving.

The mushrooms add a nice texture and a light, earthy flavor to the pasta filling.

Spinach Lasagna

Controversy abounds over which European country gets the credit for inventing lasagna—Greece or Italy. While it does get its name from a fermented ancient Greek noodle called *laganon*, credit goes to the Romans, who conquered the region in 146 BCE, for adopting the noodle into their culture and spreading its usage to Rome. Initially flatbread dough cut into thin strips and smothered in various sauces, the dish evolved over the centuries. It is believed that lasagna, more as we know it, first appeared in Naples, Italy, in the fourteenth century, where it was reserved for holidays.

Inspiration: Italy | **Serves:** 8 to 10 | **Slow cooker time:** 5 hours

INGREDIENTS

- One 14.5-ounce (411g) can diced tomatoes with basil, garlic, and oregano, drained
- One 26-ounce (737g) jar marinara sauce
- One 6-ounce (170g) can tomato paste
- 1 teaspoon (5mL) olive oil
- ½ cup (75g) chopped sweet onions, like Vidalia
- 8 ounces (227g) button or baby portobello mushrooms, sliced
- 2 teaspoon minced garlic
- One 16-ounce (454g) bag frozen chopped spinach, slightly thawed
- One 16-ounce (454g) container smooth and creamy cottage cheese
- One 8-ounce (227g) package shredded mozzarella cheese
- 1 large egg, beaten
- ½ teaspoon salt
- ¼ teaspoon pepper
- One 8-ounce (227g) package no-cook flat (not curly-edged) lasagna noodles
- ½ cup (45g) grated Parmesan cheese

1. In a large bowl, mix together the diced tomatoes, marinara sauce, and tomato paste. Set the mixture aside.

2. Heat the oil in a large nonstick skillet over medium heat. Add the onions, mushrooms, and garlic and sauté them, stirring frequently, for 3 minutes. Add the spinach and sauté, stirring frequently, until the liquid has cooked off, about 3 minutes more.

3. Remove the skillet from the heat and place the spinach mixture in a large bowl. Add the cottage cheese, shredded mozzarella, egg, salt, and pepper and stir to mix thoroughly.

4. Spread 1 cup (240mL) of the marinara sauce in the bottom of a slow cooker and top it with a complete covering of lasagna noodles. (Break the noodles to fit all spaces, overlapping them if necessary.) Spread ¾ cup (180mL) of the sauce over noodles. Top the sauce with half the spinach mixture, spreading it evenly with the back of a spoon. Place another layer of lasagna noodles over the spinach mixture. Spread ¾ cup (180mL) of the sauce on top of the noodles, then spread the remaining spinach mixture over the sauce. Add a final layer of noodles and top it with the remaining tomato sauce. Sprinkle Parmesan cheese over the sauce.

5. Cover the slow cooker and cook on the low setting for 5 hours, until the noodles are tender and the lasagna holds together when tested with a knife.

When assembling this incredibly easy lasagna, remember this little refrain: Sauce, noodles, sauce, spinach, noodles, sauce, spinach, noodles, sauce.

This rich lasagna is a perfect vegetarian main course—hearty and healthy.

Layer the lasagna in
this easy order: meat sauce,
noodles, meat sauce, cheese
mixture, noodles, meat sauce,
cheese mixture, noodles,
meat sauce, cheese mixture,
noodles, meat sauce.

This lasagna has an unexpectedly fiery zing to it because of the chilies and salsa.

Mexicana Lasagna

Far from a culture clash, this lasagna combines Mexican spiciness with the cheesy comfort of Italian cheeses. The no-cook lasagna noodles hold up better in a slow cooker than Mexican tortillas. Top each serving with sour cream, if desired. It will calm the heat of the spicy chilis.

Inspiration: Mexico and Italy | **Serves:** 6 to 8 | **Slow cooker time:** 5 hours

INGREDIENTS

- 1 tablespoon (15mL) olive oil
- 1 pound (454g) ground beef
- 1 cup (150g) chopped sweet onions, like Vidalia
- 1 teaspoon minced garlic
- 2 tablespoons (30g) taco seasoning
- ½ teaspoon salt
- Two 10-ounce (284g) cans diced tomatoes and green chilies, with juices (I used Ro-Tel)
- One 16-ounce (454g) jar medium tomatillo salsa
- One 15-ounce (425g) container part-skim ricotta cheese
- Two 8-ounce (227g) packages shredded mozzarella cheese
- 1 egg, beaten
- One 9-ounce (255g) package flat no-cook lasagna noodles
- ½ cup (45g) grated Parmesan cheese
- Sour cream

1. Heat the oil in a large nonstick skillet over medium heat. Add the ground beef, onions, and garlic. Cook the mixture, stirring frequently, until the beef has browned completely, about 5 minutes. Drain the beef mixture in a colander. Return the mixture to the skillet. Stir in the taco seasoning, salt, diced tomatoes, and salsa. Reduce the heat to low and cook, stirring occasionally, for 10 minutes. Transfer the beef mixture to a large bowl.

2. Place the ricotta and mozzarella cheeses in a medium bowl. Add the egg and stir until everything is well blended.

3. Spread 1 cup (250mL) of the meat sauce in the bottom of a 4-quart (3.8L) slow cooker. Break three dried lasagna noodles into pieces and place them in an overlapping layer on top of the meat sauce. Spread 1 cup (250mL) of the meat sauce on top of the noodles. Using two teaspoons, place one-third of the cheese mixture in dollops on top of the sauce. Spread it into an even layer with the back of the teaspoon.

4. Repeat the layers two more times: three noodles, broken in pieces; 1 cup (250mL) of the meat sauce; and one-third of the cheese mixture; three noodles, broken in pieces; 1 cup (250mL) of the meat sauce; and the final one-third of the cheese mixture.

5. Top the final layer of cheese mixture with a layer of three more noodles, broken in pieces. Spread the remaining meat sauce on top of the noodles. Sprinkle Parmesan cheese over the meat sauce.

6. Cover the slow cooker and cook on the low setting for 5 hours, or until the noodles are cooked through and the lasagna layers hold together when tested with a sharp knife. (You can hold the lasagna on the warm setting for up to 30 minutes.)

7. Cut the lasagna into wedges and serve it immediately with sour cream on the side.

Mac 'n' Cheese with Caramelized Onions and Tomatoes

Almost lasagna, this slow-cooked macaroni and cheese redefines the original concept from the 1950s, elevating good old Velveeta® cheese to create a dish that pleases the adult palate.

Inspiration: USA | **Serves:** 8 to 10 | **Slow cooker time:** 3½ to 4 hours

INGREDIENTS

- ½ tablespoon (7g) margarine
- 1 pound (454g) elbow macaroni or penne rigate pasta
- One 28-ounce (794g) can crushed tomatoes with herbs
- 2 tablespoons (28g) butter, divided
- 2 large sweet onions, like Vidalia, cut in half and thinly sliced
- 1 teaspoon sugar
- Two 12-ounce (340g) cans evaporated milk
- 1 teaspoon salt
- ½ teaspoon pepper
- 1 pound (454g) processed cheese (I used Velveeta), cut into 1-inch (2.5 cm) chunks
- 2 eggs, beaten
- Parmesan cheese

1. Liberally grease the bottom and sides of a 6-quart (5.7L) slow cooker with the margarine. Place the uncooked pasta and tomatoes in the slow cooker and stir to combine them.

2. Melt the butter in a large nonstick skillet over medium heat. Add the onions, then sprinkle them with sugar and sauté them, stirring occasionally, for 5 minutes. Reduce the heat to medium-low and continue sautéing the onions until they are soft and caramelized, about 15 minutes more. Transfer the onions to the slow cooker and stir to combine the ingredients.

3. Place the evaporated milk, salt, pepper, and cheese in a large saucepan over medium-low heat. Cook the mixture, stirring frequently, until the cheese has melted. Do not allow the cheese sauce to boil.

4. Remove the sauce from the heat and pour it into the slow cooker. Stir to combine the ingredients. Allow the mixture to cool for 5 minutes, then stir in the beaten eggs.

5. Cover the slow cooker and cook on the low setting for 3½ to 4 hours, until the pasta has cooked through but is not mushy, and the cheese sauce has thickened.

6. To serve, cut the mac 'n' cheese into wedges and serve each portion sprinkled with Parmesan cheese.

Only evaporated milk and processed cheese can withstand a long, slow cooking process without curdling.

The beaten eggs act as a thickening agent. You must allow the cheese sauce mixture to cool for a few minutes before adding the eggs so that they won't cook when stirred into the macaroni and cheese sauce.

Rich and textural, this mac 'n' cheese is served cut into wedges.

Ziti captures the rich, smooth pumpkin sauce within its tubes.

Chardonnay Pumpkin-Sausage Sauce

Pumpkins are mature winter squash that are native to North America. They are one of the oldest domesticated plants going back as far as 7000 BCE. Perfect for Halloween night supper over a steaming plate of ziti pasta, this pumpkin sauce is smooth, rich, and flavorful.

Inspiration: North America | **Makes:** 8 cups (1.9L) | **Slow cooker time:** 3½ hours

INGREDIENTS

- 1 pound (454g) Italian sausage, casings removed
- ¼ teaspoon crushed red pepper flakes
- 1 cup (150g) chopped sweet onions, like Vidalia
- 10 cloves garlic, thinly sliced
- 1 tablespoon snipped fresh sage or 1 teaspoon dried sage leaves
- One 15-ounce (425g) can pumpkin puree
- ½ cup (120mL) chardonnay wine
- 1½ cups (360mL) chicken broth
- ½ teaspoon salt
- ⅛ teaspoon ground cinnamon
- 1 tablespoon (12g) sugar

1. Place the sausage and red pepper flakes in a large nonstick skillet over medium heat. Cook the sausage for 2 minutes, breaking it into small pieces with a wooden spoon. Add the onions and garlic and sauté the mixture, stirring frequently, for 2 more minutes. Transfer the sausage mixture to a 4-quart (3.8L) slow cooker.

2. Add the pumpkin puree, wine, broth, salt, cinnamon, and sugar to the slow cooker. Stir until all the ingredients are well combined and smooth.

3. Cover the slow cooker and cook on the low setting for 3½ hours. Serve the sauce immediately over ziti pasta or transfer it to covered containers and refrigerate or freeze it until needed.

If you want to be truly adventurous by trying to make your own pumpkin puree, stick with smaller sugary pumpkins.

Sausage Puttanesca Sauce

Puttanesca—salty, pungent, and fresh—means "streetwalker" style, which gives a tantalizing clue as to its Italian origins. Serve this tasty sauce with your choice of pasta or use it in lasagna. You can double the recipe and use a 6-quart (5.7mL) slow cooker. The cooking time remains the same.

Inspiration: Italy | **Makes:** 6 cups (1.4L) | **Slow cooker time:** 7 hours

INGREDIENTS

- 1 tablespoon (15mL) olive oil
- 2 teaspoons minced garlic
- 1 pound (454g) hot Italian sausage
- One 28-ounce (794g) can whole peeled plum tomatoes, drained and roughly chopped
- Two 14.5-ounce (411g) cans petite-diced tomatoes, drained
- ¼ cup (45g) capers, rinsed and drained
- 2 tablespoons (23g) pitted and chopped oil-cured kalamata olives
- ¼ teaspoon salt
- 2 tablespoons (28g) Italian herb paste (I used Gourmet Garden Italian Herbs Stir-In Paste) or 1 teaspoon dried oregano and 1 teaspoon dried basil

1. Place the olive oil in a large nonstick skillet over medium heat. When the oil is hot, add the garlic and sauté it for 30 seconds. Add the sausage and use a wooden spoon to break it into bits. Cook, stirring frequently, until the meat is cooked through.

2. Use a slotted spoon to remove the sausage and drain it on paper towels. Transfer the sausage and garlic to a 4-quart (3.8L) slow cooker.

3. Add the tomatoes, capers, olives, salt, and herb paste to the slow cooker. Stir to combine the ingredients. Cover the slow cooker and cook on the low setting for 5½ hours. Stir the ingredients, re-cover, and then cook an additional 1½ hours.

4. Serve the sauce over your choice of pasta or transfer it to covered containers and refrigerate or freeze until needed.

You'll find oil-cured kalamata olives where you'd find regular jarred olives in your supermarket. They are olives that have been cured in oil and look black and shriveled. Kalamata olives have a distinctively pungent flavor. Once opened, store the olives in the refrigerator. They will keep for up to 6 months.

The combination of capers and kalamata olives imparts a salty, pungent vibe to the Puttanesca sauce.

Veal adds a more delicate flavor to the Bolognese than beef would, but either works in this recipe.

Veal and Mushroom Bolognese Sauce

Whereas *Spaghetti alla Bolognese* is a popular Italian dish around the globe, in Bologna itself, the meaty sauce would never be served with spaghetti—a durum wheat pasta found nearer to Naples. True Bolognese sauce traditionally would be served with an egg noodle, like tagliatelle.

Inspiration: Italy | **Makes:** 6 cups (1.4L) | **Slow cooker time:** 8 hours

INGREDIENTS

- ½ ounce (14g) dried mushrooms, like chanterelles
- ¼ cup (55g) finely diced bacon
- 1 teaspoon garlic paste or finely minced garlic
- 1 cup (150g) chopped sweet onions, like Vidalia
- 1 cup (225g) finely chopped celery
- ⅓ cup (50g) finely chopped baby carrots
- 1 pound (454g) ground veal
- One 8-ounce (227g) can tomato sauce with basil, garlic, and oregano
- One 14.5-ounce (411g) can diced tomatoes with basil, garlic, and oregano with juices
- ½ cup (120mL) dry red wine
- ¾ teaspoon salt
- ¼ teaspoon ground allspice
- ⅛ teaspoon black pepper

1. Place the mushrooms in a medium bowl. Pour 1 cup (240mL) of warm water over the mushrooms and allow them to soak for 30 minutes.

2. Meanwhile, place the bacon in a large nonstick skillet over medium heat. Cook the bacon for 1 minute, stirring constantly. Add the onions, celery, and carrots to the skillet and sauté them for 2 minutes, stirring frequently. Add the veal and sauté the mixture, stirring frequently, until the meat is browned, about 3 minutes.

3. Transfer the veal mixture to a 4-quart (3.8L) slow cooker. Add the tomato sauce, diced tomatoes with juices, wine, salt, allspice, and pepper to the slow cooker. Stir until the ingredients are well combined.

4. Drain the mushrooms in a medium sieve. Rinse the mushrooms and drain them again. Add the mushrooms to the slow cooker and stir to combine them.

5. Cover the slow cooker and cook on the low setting for 8 hours. Serve immediately atop the pasta of your choice or transfer the sauce to a covered container and refrigerate or freeze it until needed.

Dried chanterelles are excellent sources of fiber and calcium. They can be expensive because of their scarcity, but the flavor is worth the cost.

Mushroom, Tomato, and Artichoke Sauce

This hearty meatless sauce is great tossed with cheese tortellini or tubular pasta like penne. It also makes a tasty Italian-style topping for grilled chicken or fish.

Inspiration: Italy | **Makes:** 8 cups (1.9L) | **Slow cooker time:** 4 hours

INGREDIENTS

- 1 tablespoon (15mL) olive oil
- 1 cup (150g) chopped sweet onions, like Vidalia
- 2 teaspoons garlic paste or finely minced garlic
- Two 10-ounce (284g) packages fresh button mushrooms, wiped clean and sliced

- Two 14-ounces (397g) cans artichoke hearts, drained and chopped
- 2 tablespoons (15g) capers, rinsed and drained
- One 2.25-ounce (64g) can sliced ripe olives, drained

- Two 14.5-ounce (411g) cans diced fire-roasted tomatoes with garlic and juices
- One 8-ounce (227g) can tomato sauce with basil, garlic, and oregano
- ¼ cup (60mL) white wine

1. Place the oil in a large nonstick skillet over medium heat. Add the onions and garlic and sauté them, stirring constantly, for 1 minute. Add the mushrooms and sauté them, stirring frequently, for 4 minutes. Transfer the mushroom mixture to a 4-quart (3.8L) slow cooker.

2. Add the chopped artichokes, capers, olives, diced tomatoes, tomato sauce, and wine. Stir to combine the ingredients. Cover the slow cooker and cook on the low setting for 4 hours.

3. Transfer 3 cups (720mL) of the sauce to a blender and puree it until it's smooth. Return the puree to the slow cooker and stir it into the sauce. Serve the sauce immediately atop the pasta of your choice or transfer it to covered containers and refrigerate or freeze it until needed.

Artichokes have been enjoyed by humans for thousands of years, and with good reason: out of all the vegetables, only beans have more antioxidants.

The tortellini hollows capture this vibrant meatless sauce.

Bell pepper lovers, alert! This recipe showcases the members of the capsicum family in a flavorful Sicilian vegetable stew.

Peperonata

This classic Sicilian vegetable stew can be served over short tubular pasta, like penne, atop crusty bread, like bruschetta, or as a side dish accompaniment for grilled spicy Italian sausage or vegetarian sausage.

Inspiration: Italy | **Serves:** 8 to 10 | **Slow cooker time:** 3 hours

INGREDIENTS

- 3 tablespoons (45mL) olive oil, divided
- 2 red onions, halved and thinly sliced
- 1 tablespoon (14g) garlic paste or finely minced garlic
- 1 tablespoon (14g) Italian herb paste (I used Gourmet Garden Italian Herbs Stir-In Paste)
- 2 large red bell peppers, cored, seeded, and cut into thin strips
- 2 large yellow bell peppers, cored, seeded, and cut into thin strips
- 2 large orange bell peppers, cored, seeded, and cut into thin strips
- 10 large plum tomatoes, seeded and chopped
- ¼ cup (45g) capers, rinsed and drained
- 1 tablespoon (15mL) plus 1 teaspoon (5mL) red wine vinegar
- Salt and black pepper
- 1 teaspoon Fox Point Seasoning (see the tip box below), optional
- ¾ cup (15g) snipped fresh basil

1. Place 2 tablespoons (30mL) of the oil in a large nonstick skillet over medium heat. Add the onions and sauté them for 7 minutes, stirring frequently. Add the garlic and herb pastes and sauté the mixture for 1 minute, stirring constantly. Transfer the onion mixture to a 5½-quart (5.2L) slow cooker.

2. Place the remaining 1 tablespoon (15mL) of oil in the skillet. Add the peppers and sauté them for 3 minutes, stirring frequently, until they have softened. Transfer the peppers to the slow cooker.

3. Add the tomatoes, capers, vinegar, 2 teaspoons (12g) of the salt, 1 teaspoon (2g) of the black pepper, and the Fox Point Seasoning to the slow cooker. Stir to combine the ingredients.

4. Cover the slow cooker and cook on the low setting for 3 hours, until the peppers have cooked through but are not mushy. Stir in the basil and add salt and pepper to taste.

5. Serve the peperonata immediately or transfer it to a covered container and refrigerate it until needed. (Reheat it gently in a large nonstick saucepan over low heat before serving.)

Fox Point Seasoning is a great combination of salt, dried shallots, dried chives, garlic powder, onion powder, and ground green peppercorns. You can make up your own blend of these spices if you don't want to order the Fox Point Seasoning.

> Both Goya and Badia brands make a sazón blend of coriander, annatto, salt, garlic, dehydrated onion, paprika, and other Spanish spices. It usually can be found in the Spanish section of your supermarket, at Spanish groceries, or through online retailers.

These flavorful black beans are versatile—eat them on their own, serve over rice, fill a tortilla—the options are endless.

Cuban Black Beans

Frijoles negros, or black beans, are a staple in Cuba as well as other islands of the Caribbean. Cubans often serve the beans topped with a cupful of hot yellow rice. Dried black beans must be picked through carefully to remove discolored or misshapen ones and then rinsed thoroughly. The beans should be soaked for at least 10 hours to re-hydrate them before they are cooked.

Inspiration: Cuba | **Serves:** 8 to 10 | **Slow cooker time:** 6 hours

INGREDIENTS

- One 14-ounce (397g) package dried black beans
- 1½ teaspoons salt, divided
- 2 tablespoons (30mL) olive oil
- 2 cups (300g) chopped sweet onions, like Vidalia
- 2 cups (350g) chopped green bell peppers
- 4 teaspoons garlic paste or finely minced garlic
- 1 teaspoon dried marjoram
- ¼ teaspoon black pepper
- 1 teaspoon sugar
- ½ teaspoon (2.5mL) cider vinegar
- 1 packet sazón (I use Goya or Badia, see the tip box above)
- 2 bay leaves

1. One day ahead, sort through the beans, discarding any broken ones. Rinse and drain the beans, then place them in a large bowl. Add enough water to cover the beans by 3 inches (7.6cm). Cover the bowl with plastic wrap and allow the beans to soak at room temperature overnight.

2. To cook, place the beans and soaking water in a 5- to 5½-quart (4.8 to 5.2L) slow cooker. Add 1 teaspoon of the salt. Cover the slow cooker and cook on the high setting for 3 hours, until the beans are tender. (Test the tenderness by pinching a bean between your thumb and index finger. If the bean feels soft and it splits when pinched, it is done.)

3. Drain the beans in a colander, reserving 1 cup (240mL) of the cooking liquid. Return the beans to the slow cooker.

4. Place the olive oil in a large nonstick skillet over medium heat. When the oil is hot, add the onions, green peppers, garlic, marjoram, ½ teaspoon of the salt, pepper, sugar, vinegar, and sazón seasoning. Sauté the mixture, stirring frequently, for 4 to 5 minutes or until the onions and peppers soften and the mixture is fragrant.

5. Transfer the vegetable mixture to the slow cooker. Add the bay leaves and reserved cooking liquid, then stir until the ingredients are well mixed.

6. Re-cover the slow cooker and cook on the low setting for 3 more hours. Remove the bay leaves before serving. Adjust the seasoning by adding salt and pepper to taste.

Moros y Cristianos

Moros y Cristianos translates literally to Moors and Christians and it is a dish of black beans and rice that is a staple of Cuban cuisine and the cuisines of other Latin and South American countries. The name is said to date back to a time between the eighth and fifteenth centuries when the Islamic Moors and the Christian Spaniards battled for occupation of the Iberian Peninsula. The black beans represented the Moors and the white rice represented the Christians. The combination of beans and rice represents how the two groups eventually came to peacefully coexist.

Cuban black beans and rice are cooked separately, then served together—different from rice and beans, where the rice and beans are combined prior to cooking.

Persian Rice

Unlike conventional rice preparations, Persian rice is first boiled, then rinsed and drained, and finally slowly steamed until each individual grain is fluffy and the bottom layer of rice is golden brown. Traditionally the rice, which Iranians call *chelow*, is inverted onto a platter, like an upside-down cake. In Persian households, the crisp, golden-brown crust, known as *tahdig* (pronounced tah-deeg), that tops the rice "cake" is the most coveted part of the meal.

Inspiration: Iran | **Serves:** 12 to 16 | **Slow cooker time:** 2 hours

INGREDIENTS
- 3 cups (534g) basmati rice
- 2 teaspoons salt
- 2 tablespoons (28g) butter
- 10 threads saffron, ground with mortar and pestle

1. Place the rice in a nonstick, stovetop-safe, 5½-quart (5.2L) slow cooker insert. Cover the rice with water and, with your hands, agitate the rice to release the starch. Pour off the cloudy water and repeat this process until the water is clear. Pour off the water a final time, then add enough cold water to cover the rice by 3 inches (7.6cm).

2. Cover the slow cooker insert and place it on a burner over high heat. Bring the rice and water to a rolling boil (keep an eye on this as it can boil over quickly). Reduce the heat to medium, remove the cover, and boil the rice, stirring occasionally, until it softens, starts to puff, and is al dente, about 5 to 7 minutes.

3. While the rice cooks, dissolve the saffron in 2 tablespoons (30mL) of hot water.

4. Remove the insert from the heat and drain the rice in a colander. Rinse the drained rice with cold water and drain it again.

5. Wipe out the insert with paper towels to remove any starch residue and return it to the burner over medium heat. Add the butter. When the butter is melted, stir in the saffron water and add the drained rice to the pot. Use the handle of a wooden spoon to poke five holes in the rice, down to the bottom of the pan.

6. Once steam rises from the holes you made in step 5, transfer the insert to the slow cooker. Place three pieces of paper towels atop the slow cooker insert, making sure all the edges are covered. Cover the slow cooker and press down on the lid to ensure that the slow cooker is sealed completely. Steam on the low setting for 2 hours. (You can hold the rice on the warm setting for up to 2 hours, if needed.)

7. To serve, remove the insert from the slow cooker. Remove the lid and paper towels. Place a large platter over the insert. Gripping both the handles and the platter, upend the contents of the insert onto the platter. The rice will be held together in a large cake by the crispy covering of tahdig.

If you don't have a stovetop-safe slow cooker, boil the rice in a large nonstick saucepan. Place the melted butter and saffron water in a conventional 5½-quart (5.2L) slow cooker, add the prepared rice, and proceed with the directions as written.

Persian rice is the perfect accompaniment for many of the saucy dishes throughout the book.

The braised fennel imparts a subtle anise or licorce flavor.

Braised Fennel Ragout

An oft-forgotten vegetable in the United States, fennel is used extensively in European cuisines, especially those of France and Italy. It is packed with nutrients and offers a subtle licorice or anise flavor. The texture of braised fennel resembles cooked celery. Use the feathery leaves as an herbal seasoning, just as you would use dill leaves.

Inspiration: Italy | **Serves:** 4 to 6 | **Slow cooker time:** 3 to 3½ hours

INGREDIENTS

- 1 large fennel bulb
- 1 tablespoon (15mL) olive oil
- 2 teaspoons garlic paste or finely minced garlic
- 1 cup (100g) thinly sliced sweet onions, like Vidalia
- 5 large plum tomatoes, thinly sliced lengthwise, then cut in half lengthwise
- 2 tablespoons (30mL) white wine
- 1 tablespoon (15mL) honey
- 1 tablespoon (15mL) orange juice concentrate, thawed
- 1 teaspoon salt
- ½ teaspoon black pepper

1. Cut the stalks off the fennel bulb and discard them. Cut the fennel bulb crosswise into ½-inch (1.5cm) slices. Remove the small green center root from each slice and discard it. Discard the root end of the bulb. Place the fennel slices in a colander, rinse them with cold water, and dry them with paper towels.

2. Place the oil in a large nonstick skillet over medium heat. When the oil is hot, add the sliced fennel, garlic, and onions. Sauté the mixture for 3 minutes, stirring frequently. Add the tomatoes, wine, honey, orange juice concentrate, salt, and pepper. Sauté the mixture for 2 minutes more, stirring frequently.

3. Transfer the fennel mixture to a 1½-quart (1.4L) slow cooker. Cover the slow cooker and cook on the low setting for 3 to 3½ hours, until the fennel is tender. Serve immediately.

Fennel's subtle flavor is herbaceous and refreshing, and the vegetable offers numerous health benefits.

Black-Eyed Peas with Tomatoes, Mushrooms, and Onions

If you thought black-eyed peas were only served in the American South, think again. A popular dish served in India, these black-eyed peas (called *lobia* in Hindi) are delicately yet pungently seasoned with cumin, coriander, and turmeric—ubiquitous herbs and spices of the region. Serve it as a vegetarian main dish or with the Indian beef stew known as Rogan Josh (see the recipe on page 50).

Inspiration: India | **Serves:** 8 | **Slow cooker time:** 10 to 12½ hours

INGREDIENTS

- 1¾ cups (455g) dried black-eyed peas
- One 32-ounce (1L) carton mushroom broth
- 1 cup (240mL) water
- 3 tablespoons (45mL) canola oil
- One 1-inch (2.5cm) stick cinnamon
- 1 teaspoon cumin seeds
- 4 teaspoons (18g) garlic paste or finely minced garlic
- 2 cups (300g) chopped sweet onions, like Vidalia
- 2 cups (150g) sliced button mushrooms
- 2 cups (300g) quartered cherry tomatoes
- 2 teaspoons dried coriander leaves
- ½ teaspoon ground cumin
- ½ teaspoon turmeric
- ¼ teaspoon cayenne pepper
- 2 teaspoons salt
- 3 tablespoons (9g) snipped fresh parsley or cilantro

1. The day before, pick over the dried peas, discarding any broken ones. Place the peas in a medium bowl and add enough water to cover the peas by 3 inches (7.6cm). Set them aside at room temperature to soak overnight.

2. Early in the morning, drain the peas in a colander, rinse them with cold water, and drain them again. Transfer the peas to a 4-quart (3.8L) slow cooker. Add the mushroom broth and 1 cup (240mL) of the water. Cover the slow cooker and cook on the low setting for 8 to 10 hours, until the peas are al dente. Drain the peas in a colander, then return them to the slow cooker.

3. Place the oil, cinnamon stick, and cumin seeds in a large nonstick skillet over medium heat. When the oil starts to sizzle, add the garlic and onions. Sauté them until the onions have softened, stirring occasionally, for about 3 minutes. Add the mushrooms and sauté the mixture for 3 minutes more, stirring occasionally.

4. Add the tomatoes, coriander, ground cumin, turmeric, cayenne, and salt, then stir to combine. Reduce the heat to low and cook for 8 more minutes, stirring occasionally. Transfer the tomato mixture to the slow cooker and stir until the ingredients are well combined.

5. Cover the slow cooker and cook on the low setting for 2 to 2½ hours, until the black-eyed peas are tender. Remove the cinnamon stick, sprinkle the black-eyed peas with fresh parsley or cilantro, and serve immediately.

Be sure to use dried coriander leaves, not ground coriander. If you can't find mushroom broth, substitute vegetable broth. If you can't find cumin seeds, substitute ½ teaspoon of ground cumin.

These black-eyed peas feature a sophisticated blend of spices.

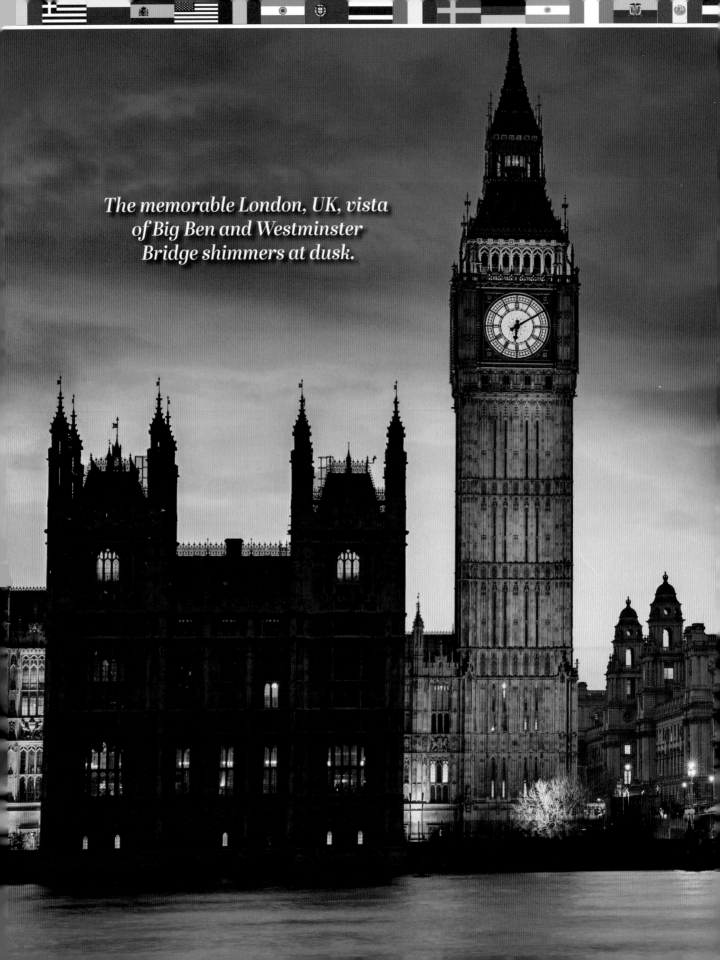

The memorable London, UK, vista of Big Ben and Westminster Bridge shimmers at dusk.

DESSERTS

Baking indulgent desserts can often feel like a complicated, daunting process, but the simple combination of fruit and slow cooker makes it all seem effortless!

ALL INCLUDED DESSERT RECIPES ARE VEGETARIAN

Strawberry-Blueberry Crumble

Summertime, summertime . . . Serve this scrumptious berry crumble with a dollop of whipped cream or a scoop of vanilla ice cream. Although a little decadent, it is also fantastic for breakfast!

Inspiration: North America | **Serves:** 8 | **Slow cooker time:** 2 hours

INGREDIENTS

- 8 tablespoons (113g) butter, softened at room temperature
- ½ cup (100g) plus ⅔ cup (135g) light brown sugar, divided
- ¼ teaspoon ground cinnamon
- ½ teaspoon salt, divided
- ⅔ cup (65g) quick oats
- ¾ cup (90g) flour, divided
- 4 cups (800g) sliced strawberries, washed and patted dry with paper towels
- 2 dry pints (680g) blueberries, washed and patted dry with paper towels
- 1 teaspoon grated lemon peel
- 1 teaspoon (5mL) fresh lemon juice

1. Up to 8 hours ahead, place the butter, ½ cup (100g) of the brown sugar, cinnamon, and ¼ teaspoon of the salt in a medium bowl. Beat the mixture with an electric hand mixer or stir with a spoon until it's smooth. Add the oats and ½ cup (60g) of the flour and beat or stir until the ingredients are well mixed. Cover this topping mixture with plastic wrap and refrigerate until needed.

2. Place the berries in a large bowl. Mix ⅔ cup (135g) of the brown sugar, ¼ cup (30g) of the flour, and ¼ teaspoon of the salt together in a medium bowl. Add the sugar mixture to the berries and toss them gently with a large spoon until the berries are well coated. Stir the grated lemon peel and lemon juice into the berries.

3. Transfer the berry mixture to a 4-quart (3.8L) slow cooker. Remove the topping mixture from the refrigerator and, using clean hands, crumble the topping evenly over the fruit. Cover the slow cooker insert with plastic wrap and refrigerate until needed.

4. To cook, remove the insert from the refrigerator and allow the berry mixture to sit at room temperature for 30 minutes. Remove the plastic wrap and place the insert in the slow cooker, then cover it and cook on the low setting for 2 hours.

5. When the berry mixture is bubbly, serve immediately, or reduce the heat setting to warm and hold the crumble for up to 1 hour.

Placing the topping in the refrigerator while you prepare the berry filling allows the butter in the topping to firm up a little, making it easier to crumble over the berries.

This crumble showcases berry season.

This apple crisp tastes just like apple pie, but with a streusel-like coating.

Apple Crisp

You don't need to wait for apple season to make this classic dessert.
Granny Smith apples are available all year long.

Inspiration: North America and Great Britain | **Serves:** 6 | **Slow cooker time:** 3½ hours

INGREDIENTS

- 5 large Granny Smith apples, peeled, cored, and sliced
- ¼ cup (60mL) melted butter, divided
- 1 teaspoon grated lemon peel
- 1 tablespoon grated orange peel
- 2 tablespoons (30mL) orange liqueur (I used Grand Marnier)
- 2 tablespoons (30mL) almond liqueur (I used Amaretto)
- One 3.4-ounce (96g) package French vanilla instant pudding mix (I used Jell-O)
- 1 teaspoon ground cinnamon
- ½ cup (40g) chopped vanilla wafer cookies (I used Nilla Wafers)
- ¼ cup (27g) slivered almonds
- ¼ cup (50g) sugar

1. Place the apple slices in a large bowl. Pour 2 tablespoons (30mL) of the melted butter over the apples and toss them to combine. Sprinkle the grated lemon and orange peels and both liqueurs over the apples and toss them to combine. In a separate medium bowl, mix the pudding mix and cinnamon together. Add the mixture to the apples in thirds, tossing to combine the ingredients between each addition.

2. Transfer the apple mixture to a 4- or 5-quart (3.8 or 4.8L) slow cooker. Cover the slow cooker and cook on the low heat setting for 3½ hours, until the apples are soft and the mixture is bubbly. Reduce the heat setting to warm and hold for up to 1 hour.

3. Meanwhile, place the remaining 2 tablespoons (30mL) of the melted butter in a small nonstick skillet over low heat. Add the vanilla wafer cookie crumbs, almonds, and sugar. Cook the mixture, stirring constantly, for 1½ minutes. Remove the skillet from the heat and allow the mixture to cool in the skillet, stirring occasionally.

4. To serve, place a portion of the apple crisp in a shallow dessert bowl. Sprinkle the almond-crumb mixture over the apples and serve immediately.

An apple peeler/corer machine makes fast work of the apple preparation for this recipe. You'll find them in kitchen supply stores.

Baked Sugar Apples

In the apple-producing countries of the northern hemisphere, nothing spells autumn like baked apples. Look for Pink Lady, Honeycrisp, or other sweet-tart varieties at your local farmers market.

Inspiration: Northern Hemisphere | **Serves:** 4 | **Slow cooker time:** 5 hours

INGREDIENTS

- 2 tablespoons (28g) butter, melted
- 4 medium sweet-tart apples, washed, peeled, and cored
- ½ cup (100g) white granulated sugar or demerara sugar
- 6 tablespoons (90mL) apricot preserves, divided
- Ice cream

1. Brush the inside of a 2-quart (1.9L) slow cooker with butter. Brush each apple with melted butter, working one apple at a time. Place the sugar in a shallow bowl, then roll each buttered apple in the sugar.

2. Place each apple in the slow cooker. Spoon 1½ tablespoons (22.5mL) of apricot preserves into the cored center cavities of each apple. Sprinkle any remaining sugar atop the apples in the slow cooker.

3. Cover the slow cooker and cook on the low setting for 5 hours, until the apples are soft, cooked through, and lightly browned. (You can keep the apples in the slow cooker on the warm setting for up to 2 hours.)

4. To serve, place one apple on each of four dessert plates. Place a scoop of your favorite ice cream next to each apple and serve immediately.

Demerara sugar is a light brown sugar with large golden crystals. You can usually find it in the sugar section of your supermarket.

Baked sugar apples also pair nicely with yogurt and granola for a slightly decadent breakfast treat.

Peach schnapps adds a little extra zing to this sweet crumble.

Peach Crumble

Desserts don't get any easier than this, a true fix-it-and-forget-it recipe. Serve it hot out of the slow cooker, topped with ice cream, frozen yogurt, or whipped cream.

Inspiration: North America and Great Britain | **Serves:** 6 | **Slow cooker time:** 4 to 4½ hours

INGREDIENTS

- ½ tablespoon (7g) margarine
- One 21-ounce (595g) can peach pie filling
- One 1-pound (454g) bag frozen sliced peaches, thawed
- 1 tablespoon (15mL) peach schnapps
- One 18.25-ounce (517g) package yellow cake mix (I used Betty Crocker Super Moist Butter Recipe Yellow cake mix)
- ¾ cup (95g) chopped pecans
- ½ cup (120mL) melted butter

1. Coat the bottom and sides of a 4-quart (3.8L) slow cooker with the margarine. Spread the pie filling in the bottom of the slow cooker. Top the pie filling with the sliced peaches. Sprinkle the schnapps over the peaches.

2. In a large bowl, stir the cake mix and pecans together. Add the melted butter and stir the mixture with a fork. Sprinkle the cake mixture over the fruit mixture in the slow cooker.

3. Cover the slow cooker and cook on the low setting for 4 to 4½ hours, until the fruit is bubbly and the cake mixture is crumbly and cooked through. Serve immediately or hold on the warm setting for up to 1 hour.

You can get creative with this recipe. Pair different pie fillings with matching fresh or frozen fruit. Sprinkle the fruit with corresponding liqueurs. For example, try matching cherry pie filling with frozen sour cherries and cherry liqueur or apple pie filling with sliced apples and almond liqueur.

Peaches were first domesticated and cultivated in ancient China, and the fruit still symbolizes springtime and longevity in Chinese culture.

Orange-Rhubarb Bread "Pud"

Cultivated rhubarb has been used medicinally in China for more than 5,000 years. Botanically considered to be a vegetable rather than a fruit, rhubarb was not widely used for culinary purposes until the early nineteenth century, when it became a popular dessert ingredient in England. The addition of oranges lifts this English bread pudding ("pud") out of the ordinary.

Inspiration: Great Britain | **Serves:** 4 | **Slow cooker time:** 3 hours

INGREDIENTS

- 1 naval orange
- 1½ to 2 cups (183 to 244g) diced rhubarb
- 1 tablespoon (12g) instant tapioca (I used Kraft Minute Tapioca)
- ¾ cup (150g) sugar
- 2 cups (100g) cubed white bread
- 3 tablespoons (45mL) melted butter
- ¼ cup (18g) unsweetened coconut
- Vanilla ice cream, optional
- Whipped cream, optional
- Heavy cream, optional

1. Grate the peel of the orange and set the grated orange zest aside. Peel the orange. Cut the orange into slices, and then into ½-inch (1.5cm) pieces, reserving any juices. Set the orange pieces and reserved juice aside.

2. Place the rhubarb, tapioca, sugar, bread cubes, melted butter, diced oranges with juices, 2 tablespoons (12g) of the grated orange zest, and coconut in a medium bowl. Stir until the ingredients are well mixed. Transfer the mixture to a 1½- or 2-quart (1.4 or 1.9L) slow cooker. (Wrap any remaining grated orange zest in plastic wrap and freeze it to use at another time.)

3. Cover the slow cooker and cook on the low setting for 3 hours. (You can hold the pudding on the warm setting for up to 1 hour.) Serve the pudding warm, with a scoop of vanilla ice cream, a dollop of whipped cream, or a splash of heavy cream.

Two stalks of rhubarb equal about 1 cup (122g) diced. To serve a larger group, double the recipe and place it in a 4-quart (3.8L) slow cooker. The cooking time remains the same. Some supermarkets sell frozen diced rhubarb. You do not need to defrost the rhubarb before using it in this recipe.

A "pud" is traditionally a homey, rustic dessert.

You can substitute dried raisins, cherries, cranberries, figs, or any other favorite dried fruits in this recipe.

Rummy Apricot-Currant Bread Pudding

The French are renowned for transforming stale bread and pantry items into stunning desserts. This bread pudding showcases rum-soaked dried fruits. The type of bread you use determines the texture of the resulting pudding: country-style, chewy bread will yield a soufflé-like pudding, while soft, dense bread will create a more compact dessert.

Inspiration: France | **Serves:** 6 to 8 | **Slow cooker time:** 4 hours

INGREDIENTS

- ½ cup (75g) dried currants
- 1 cup (190g) chopped dried apricots
- ⅓ cup (80mL) dark rum (I used Myers's), plus more for serving
- Two 12-ounce (340g) cans evaporated milk
- 3 large eggs
- 1 teaspoon (5mL) vanilla
- ⅜ teaspoon salt
- 1 cup (200g) sugar, divided
- 2 tablespoons (28g) butter, divided
- 10 slices stale bread, about ½-inch (1.5cm) thick

1. The day before, place the currants and apricots in a small bowl. Stir in the rum, cover the bowl with plastic wrap, and allow it to sit overnight at room temperature so that the dried fruits absorb the rum and plump up.

2. Early in the day, place the evaporated milk in a large bowl. Whisk in the eggs, one at a time, then whisk in the vanilla, salt, and all but 4½ tablespoons (57g) of the sugar. Set the mixture aside.

3. Drain the currants and apricots, reserving the liquid. Whisk the drained liquid into the milk mixture. Reserve 1 tablespoon (10g) of the dried fruit mixture in a separate small bowl. Set everything aside.

4. Liberally grease a 4-quart (3.8L) slow cooker with butter, then cut the remaining butter into small pieces and set them aside. Place one third of the bread slices in the bottom of the slow cooker, pressing them down so that the bread covers the entire surface. Sprinkle the bread slices with one-third of the dried fruit. Pour one-third of the milk mixture over the fruit and bread. Repeat the layers two more times: bread, fruit, milk.

5. Mix the remaining sugar and reserved dried fruit together and sprinkle the mixture over the pudding. Dot the top of the pudding with the small pieces of butter.

6. Cover the slow cooker and cook on the low setting for 4 hours, or until a knife inserted in the center comes out clean.

7. To serve, top each warm bread pudding portion with a drizzle of rum.

Brandied Vanilla Bean Applesauce

New Englanders consider Macoun apples to be the best around. Most often found at farmers markets, roadside stands, or specialty markets, Macouns are available only in October and November. If you find them, buy a peck or two to make this great dessert applesauce. You can also substitute another sweet-tart crisp variety of apple.

Inspiration: North America | **Makes:** 4 cups (946mL) | **Slow cooker time:** 4 hours

INGREDIENTS

- 2 cups (480mL) apple juice
- 10 sweet-tart apples, like Macoun, Jonagold, or Honeycrisp
- 3 tablespoons (42g) butter, melted
- 4 tablespoons (48g) sugar
- 2 tablespoons (30mL) brandy
- ½ vanilla bean, cut lengthwise

1. Place the apple juice in a large bowl. Peel, core, and thinly slice the apples. Place the slices in the bowl of apple juice, then drain the slices in a colander, reserving 3 tablespoons (45mL) of the apple juice.

2. Return the apple slices to the empty bowl. Add the reserved apple juice, butter, sugar, and brandy. Toss to combine the ingredients. Place the mixture in a 4- to 5-quart (3.8 to 4.7L) slow cooker. Bury the vanilla bean in the middle of the apple slices.

3. Cover the slow cooker and cook on the low setting for 4 hours, until the apples can be broken up with a wooden spoon to form a coarse sauce. Remove the vanilla bean and discard it.

4. Serve the sauce warm or refrigerate it in a covered container for up to 1 week or freeze it for up to 2 months.

The vanilla bean is the pod of the flat-leafed vanilla orchid. It is the source of vanilla flavoring.

Although great on its own, this applesauce is super as an accompaniment for pork roasts or chops, served on top of French toast, or used as a filling for crepes or puff pastry shells.

Index of Recipes by Country/Region

Index

Note: Page numbers in *italics* indicate recipes. Recipe titles followed by an asterisk (*) indicate vegetarian dishes. Page numbers in **bold** indicate photos of international sites.

Photo Credits:

About the Author

Victoria Shearer wore several professional hats—elementary school teacher, advertising agency account executive, cooking magazine copy editor—before combining her passion for food and travel with her love of writing. A longtime food and travel writer, for the past twenty-nine years she has written for many national magazines and newspapers. This enabled her to travel to many interesting destinations around the globe.

Vicki maintains that to really experience another culture, you have to use all your senses, chief among them taste. To that end, she has endeavored to taste her way around the world. Her most memorable tasting is easy to recall . . . sampling grilled zebra in South Africa!

Vicki is the author of ten editions of *Insiders' Guide® to Florida Keys & Key West* (Globe Pequot), as well as *Walking Places in New England* (Out There Press, 2001), *It Happened in the Florida Keys* (Globe Pequot, 2008, 2020), *Florida Keys & Key West Chef's Table* (Globe Pequot, 2014, 2022), *Florida Keys Cookbook* (Globe Pequot, 2005, 2012, 2023), and *Way Up North Wisconsin Cookbook* (Globe Pequot, 2024).

Vicki and her husband Bob divide their time between Wake Forest, North Carolina, and their cabin in Mercer, Wisconsin. No day is complete without puttering in the kitchen, but she also loves to play mah-jongg, do needlepoint, and cheer on her beloved Carolina Hurricanes hockey team. And while the title of "author" and "cook" are quite nice, Vicki's most cherished monikers are "Mom" (to Brian, Kristen, and John) and "Grammy" (to Christopher, Dona, Bethany, Bobby, Ashleigh, Leia, Nicholas, and Sammy).

Acknowledgments

Some things never change—The Beatles sang the words first, and they have rung true for every cookbook I have tackled for the past eighteen years: "I get by with a little help from my friends!" My loyal taste testers are an elite, dedicated group. My sincere gratitude goes to these willing-to-try-anything friends. Your input was invaluable. And many thanks to my long-suffering, never-complaining husband Bob, who really would have preferred a thick, grilled steak after about the fiftieth slow-cooked test recipe but hung in there with me until the final recipe conversions met my satisfaction.

A special thank you, as well, to Lauren Younker and the team at Fox Chapel Publishing who gave me the opportunity to go around the world with my slow cooker!